For God's Sake

For God's Sake

*Re-imagining Priesthood and Prayer
in a Changing Church*

edited by

Jessica Martin and Sarah Coakley

CANTERBURY
PRESS

Norwich

© The Contributors 2016

First published in 2016 by the Canterbury Press Norwich
Editorial office
3rd Floor, Invicta House
108–114 Golden Lane
London EC1Y 0TG, UK

Hymns Ancient & Modern® is a registered trademark
of Hymns Ancient and Modern Ltd

Canterbury Press is an imprint of Hymns Ancient & Modern Ltd
(a registered charity)
13A Hellesdon Park Road, Norwich,
Norfolk NR6 5DR, UK

www.canterburypress.co.uk

British Library Cataloguing in Publication data

A catalogue record for this book is available
from the British Library

978 1 84825 814 3

Typeset by Regent Typesetting
Printed and bound in Great Britain by
CPI Group (UK) Ltd, Croydon

How lovely is your dwelling place, O Lord of hosts!
My soul has a desire and longing to enter the courts of
the Lord;
my heart and my flesh rejoice in the living God.
The sparrow has found her a house
and the swallow a nest where she may lay her young:
at your altars, O Lord of hosts, my King and my God.
Blessed are they who dwell in your house:
they will always be praising you.
Blessed are those whose strength is in you,
in whose heart are the highways to Zion,
who going through the barren valley find there a spring,
and the early rains will clothe it with blessing.

Psalm 84.1–6

Contents

Acknowledgements

The editors gratefully thank the Archbishop of Canterbury's discretionary fund for financial assistance with the original conference at Lichfield Cathedral in September 2011, from which this book derives.

The authors have used the following biblical translations: NRSV, NIV, AV; and have used quotations from both *Common Worship* and the 1662 *Book of Common Prayer*.

Jessica Martin also has some personal thanks to offer.

The chapter on 'Daily Prayer' was first given as a paper at a one-day conference on prayer in the Anthropology Department of the London School of Economics in May 2014, and I am grateful to all who contributed to the very helpful discussion around it, and especially its organizer, Dr Fenella Cannell.

I have discussed the book's concerns with a number of people at different stages: most importantly, of course, with my co-editor Sarah Coakley, whose incisive and clear perceptions have been absolutely invaluable, and with Christine Smith, editor at Canterbury Press, who offered both warm encouragement and patience. Also with Fenella Cannell, Cheryl Collins, Andrew Davison, David Martin, Bernice Martin, Francis Spufford and Frankie Ward.

The time and space at Friston for writing and thinking which the Duke family offered was hugely appreciated and a great joy.

This book, whatever else it is about, is about prayer in the parish; and I owe my largest debt of thanks to those in the parishes who have prayed with me in so many different ways and guises. There are too many to name all of them, but specially affectionate and grateful thanks are due to a few. To Mrs Julie Baillie LLM, whose profound and faithful lay ministry has modelled incarnational presence in Hinxton and its surrounding villages for many years. To the Revd Tricia Newland in her commitment to contemplative prayer. To Mandy Jeffery, Margaret Malcolm and Jenny Duke, who have offered prayer and wisdom as a ministry of support and discernment. Last, to those who have accompanied me in daily prayer, the Revd Caroline Wilson, Tim Hooper, Judith Sutcliffe LLM, and the late Gordon Woolhouse. And – most important of all – the Revd Charles Miller, who taught me how to be a parish priest.

Introduction

JESSICA MARTIN

The Anglican tradition and its gifts

For God's Sake is a book about the Anglican priesthood, particularly in the contemporary parochial context. It is written at a time when – especially through the developments of the last decade – formidable challenges to the continuation of the historic parochial system have come to a head; and it is written both in critical celebration of that past and in discerning hope for the future.

At first sight *For God's Sake* may look to be a very recognizable type of book, belonging to a long tradition of writing on Church of England parochial ministry. Its contributors draw on influential modern writers and practitioners within that tradition: Michael Ramsey, W. H. Vanstone, Alan Ecclestone, Geoffrey Howard, John Pridmore.[1] Above all it is standing in the long shadow of George Herbert's *Country Parson*,[2] paying

---

1 Michael Ramsey, *The Christian Priest Today* (London: SPCK, 1972); W. H. Vanstone, *Love's Endeavour, Love's Expense* (London: DLT, 1977); Alan Ecclestone, *Yes to God* (London: DLT, 1975); Geoffrey Howard, *Dare to Break Bread* (London: DLT, 1992); John Pridmore, *The Inner-City of God* (London: Canterbury Press, 2008). The nature (and longevity) of the tradition itself means, inevitably, that these priest-practitioners are all men. This is a particularly significant issue for rural ministry, where the Herbertian model bites deepest, and where a comparatively large concentration of women are serving multi-parish benefices.

2 George Herbert, *A Priest to the Temple: or the Country Parson*, in *Herbert's Remaines*, edited by Barnabas Oley (London, 1652), multiple reprintings. Justin Lewis-Anthony's riposte, *If You Meet George Herbert on the Road, Kill Him* (London and New York: Mowbray, 2009), nevertheless reiterates a good deal of Herbert's own advice in a lively repackaging.

homage (as Ramsey himself did in *The Christian Priest Today*) to Herbert in the mode of its very chapter titles, and also in its content.

But here is the difference. We write this book conscious that we are perhaps the last children of such a tradition, seeking to see how we may be both faithful and creative in an uncertain future. How may we offer ourselves into the work of God when traditional modes of parochial priesthood seem to be breaking down? We look to discern what we are called to do in the new shape the Church must take.

We bring to that task 'something old and something new'. We offer bulletins from the front which describe what the Christian priest in *today*'s today is being and doing. The wisdom nourishing us from the tradition is the gift it offers as the world it describes falls away and dies; but we are people of resurrection, and we trust in God for renewal. We are not writing lament. We are seeking for the signs of the kingdom in the signs of the times.

Moreover, we are aware that we have been here – or somewhere like it – before. In the 1590s, just around the time that George Herbert was born, Richard Hooker prefaced his foundational work for classical Anglicanism, *Of the Laws of Ecclesiastical Polity*, as a message to a future without a Church of England:

> Though for no other cause, yet for this, that that posterity may know we have not loosely through silence permitted things to pass away as in a dream, there shall be for men's information extant thus much concerning the present state of the Church of God established amongst us, and their careful endeavour which would have upheld the same.

Hooker was wrong, at least partly: while the century that followed did indeed see the temporary abolition of the Church of England, it also proved inspirationally vital for Anglican identity, theology and spiritual insight. In the 1760s, 170 years later, the Revd Laurence Sterne wrote rather mournfully that he gave the Church of England (indeed, Christianity itself) fifty more years at the outside.[3] He was not in a position to imagine the extraordinary, oxygenating impact of the Oxford Movement on an institution at that time strangling on its own worldly ease. None of this, of course, gives us any guarantee about our own future as a Church – but it reminds us (if, as Christians, we needed reminding) that out of death unexpected new life may and does arise, for 'the one who calls us is faithful'.

The Littlemore Group

Just over ten years ago, the 'Littlemore Group' was founded by Sarah Coakley and Sam Wells, who saw an opportunity to bring together once more the lived experience of ministry with the rich and fruitful tradition of Anglican theology. They joined together practitioners (priests in parishes and vowed religious) whose identity and formation was as theologians, and they got them talking and thinking together. They observed that devotional practice and deep, thoughtful theology, those two vital manifestations of the Church's life, had drawn apart since the 1960s, and that they needed each other to thrive. The Group met in 2005 at Littlemore, J. H. Newman's parish, to 're-imagine the role of religion in the life of the nation', and out of that shared work came a book, *Praying for England* (Continuum, 2008). It reaffirmed the value of the parochial tradition, the representative nature of the parish priest – 'standing at the altar with the people on his heart', as Michael Ramsey put it – and the deep wells of *caritas* connecting prayer, place and the poor to make the Church of England and her parochial system an indispensable good for the nation as a whole. Above all, *Praying for England* argued that parochial experience was a form of lived-out theology: that the life of prayer and study of the ways of God was the bedrock of every parish calling.

---

3 Laurence Sterne, *Tristram Shandy*, VI.

The signs of the times

More than a decade later the landscape has changed – irrevocably, un-ignorably. Congregations dwindle and age; a vast percentage of priests are reaching retirement and cannot be replaced quickly or completely even if the current vocational drive meets its own targets for success. Moreover, there is a visible disconnect between national self-understanding and the Church's identity politics, most notably in the area of sexuality, though there are others: for example, in the divided opinions that exist on end-of-life ethics.

All this is happening at a point where much of the nation is 'post-Christian' – which is not to say necessarily 'secular'. The 'new atheists' are a tiny, vocal, middle-class, mostly male, mostly white, educated minority, and their day is already passing. Possibly, since the rise of a militant Islamic voice in world politics, people are more exercised about questions of faith than at any time in the last fifty years. And, even aside from this phenomenon, our society still abounds with spiritual curiosity and inchoate, dispersed beliefs; but it is no longer in easy possession of an identifiable shared Christian tradition. Community, and the desire for community, is as strong as ever, but it is no longer expressed in the same way as before; people are more inclined to join like-minded support groups, to be involved in charity (often sporting, fitness being almost a religion in itself) fundraising activities, or to line up for single-issue lobbying, than they are to join a national political party – or to support a national church.

All this means not only that our parish system struggles to find clergy to staff it, but that those who service it in other ways are in short supply – for the upkeep of financial and administrative systems, the care and maintenance of buildings, and so on. The doctrinal fundamentals of Anglican theology are little known and even the point of them not well understood. People are not culturally in a place where they are receptive to being 'told what to believe'. Although it looks as if the falling numbers are at last beginning to bottom out and in places even to climb again, the situation is nevertheless grave. The great majority of our parishes are in contingently shoved-together multiple groupings.

Parish and the wider culture

I am personally convinced by the arguments for the English parochial system – convinced enough to have left another deeply rewarding vocation in order to serve it. I am convinced by its inclusive generosity, by its commitment to areas abandoned by most other forms of civic engagement, by the profound spiritual and practical possibilities of its civic and community role. I think these still have remarkable power in allowing the Church of England to have discernible Christian influence upon our culture. The everyday ministry of the parish at its best is the kingdom leaven in the bread dough of its locality, and it is still (just about) *everywhere*, in the way that no other system is – not schools, not post offices, not hospitals, not GP medical centres, not community facilities. Just churches. I became a parish priest thinking that if one simply worked hard enough and with enough enthusiasm, if one were flexible and imaginative and generous and physically visible (it is an incarnational model), then the tradition would flourish. It would be possible to live a holy life caring for a particular community, and underpinning all this with study and prayer, the people daily 'on one's heart'.

Perhaps I missed something obvious, but six years later I know that this is not ... well, it's not true *enough*. Community goodwill is worth much, and we throw it away at our peril; but unceasing effort makes churches semi-viable without filling them. I took a funeral recently for a local woman, and half the village came. They were full of goodwill. They knew me, and I knew them. But I now know they will never come to church except at Christmas, no matter what I do. The weeping widower hugged me tight at the pub and said, laughing and crying, 'I hope I don't see you again for *years*.' One of the mourners told me that the prayers I offered were 'just the same' as the crystal healing she and her mum pursued alongside her vocation as a neo-natal nurse, and that the naming ceremony she'd had for her children was 'just the same' as the Roman Catholic christening she'd decided against for them.

People won't casually wander into Christian community and worship. The young Polish woman doing my hair at the hairdressers was wondering whether to get her baby christened. 'At home,' she said, 'of course I went to church, everyone did. I loved it, the singing, the praying. I wanted to be a nun when I was a little girl – really badly! Then I came here, and – it's not the thing everyone does. It's not normal. So I don't go to church now. I'd like to get married, too, but you don't get married here, and it's so expensive.' Lived Christian faith is 'not normal'. To do it, you have to be a little bit brave. 'I loved it when I came,' said a mum in the playground who had had her banns read, 'and I said to my sister, would you laugh at me if I started coming to church? And she said no, but ...' Repeated invitations have led to texted requests for prayer but a definite policy of avoiding all social interaction with me face to face.

Even in the comparative comfort of my small group of commuter-belt parishes, no amount of energy, no amount of expended time or imagination, can make the Church thrive on the old model utterly unchanged. And I notice, too, that those within the Church who argue most passionately against change are in positions where the cold wind is not yet blowing. Perhaps the model still works in (for example) boutique city-centre churches – though that's a gathered, not a parish model – but outside towns and cities things are dramatically different.

Anxiety and trust

In the chapters that follow, written by parish priests out of very varied national contexts, one consistent thread is *anxiety*. The word, or a cognate emotion, is mentioned by almost every contributor, both as a debilitating factor in their ministry and in the culture of the Church as a whole. All talk about distraction, about the loss of control, about the breakdown of institutions. All mark the importance of place – even in this virtual culture of ours. All look to past models, in recognition that these both give us unfamiliar sustenance and yet come from a world that is vanishing even as it sustains.

'Do not worry,' Jesus says to his disciples (Matt. 6.25). Paul tells the church at Philippi, 'The Lord is near. Do not worry about anything, but in everything by prayer and supplication with thanksgiving let your requests be known to God' (Phil. 4.5b–6). The consistent message in divine encounter, whether with an angelic messenger or the presence of God himself, is 'Do not be afraid'. The transforming voice of God speaks to the young boy in the midst of the near-empty, ramshackle Temple at Shiloh (1 Sam. 3) , and to Elijah, the last surviving prophet, lying down ready to die of despair and exhaustion (1 Kings 19). Our vocation is to trust that even in the wilderness there will be food and drink enough for the journey. A ministry built upon a foundation of prayer, upon the exploration of God's being and nature, can lean upon God's goodness. Theology and practice need each other now more urgently than ever.

Transformation

This is not the same as saying, complacently, 'OK, we'll just sit back because failure is a great Christian tradition.' There was altogether too much of that sort of sentiment in the Church of England some thirty years ago. But we were not given our gifts – including our strategic, our persuasive, our community-making talents – in order to bury them in the ground. 'Doing nothing is not an option,' as Alex Hughes quotes in this book's penultimate chapter. We *need* the new initiatives of evangelization now beginning. We need them to re-imagine and reconfigure our systems so that they assist rather than hamper the vocation to prayer, study and speaking the good news of Jesus Christ, to those around us and to those who come after.

But the systems are not themselves the answer without the deep connection of prayer; the past offers wisdom as well as stumbling blocks; and some new initiatives – particularly perhaps those that seek quick cash-crop returns without significant spiritual or theological depth in the face of institutional anxiety – come with stumbling blocks of their own.[4] In Britain we live at a time where all our social structures are built around market systems, where value has only an economic calculation attached to it, whether we are talking about schools, healthcare systems, transport, every aspect of community care, the basic welfare of children, or the *modus operandi* of political parties in often toxic relationship with the marketable aspects of media influence. But the love of Christ is not a measurable or a marketable good. It is a gift. The kingdom leaven we bring is freely offered, 'without money and without price' (Isa. 55); if we forget love, our faith and our hope have no lasting worth (1 Cor. 13). Yes, things have to be paid for. We are not in the kingdom of heaven yet. We need to be smart and flexible about how that is done. But even those systems may be built more authentically upon theologies of gift than on the conventional, unforgiving ideologies of the market.

---

4 It is for this reason that this book deliberately refuses polemics between traditional Anglican church practice and modern mission strategies.

Transition

So this is a transitional book. We are conscious that we speak from a place of uncertainty – dangerous, certainly, but also full of the excitement of possibility, of the unexpected and the new. And this is what we would expect from a perspective that continues to make prayer its non-negotiable and sustaining matrix. We believe that new springs are already arising from a renewal of the collective life of prayer and from a refreshed, more collaborative understanding of the relationship between the priest and the whole people of God. Sarah Coakley, in the book's final chapter, has more to say about the possibilities of a different model of praying community, a vision offered by Archbishop Justin's commitment to the renewal of vowed religious communities and in the continuing groundswell of the neo-monastic movement. We notice that people's readiness to think freely and openly together about matters of faith provides a fruitful place in which to offer the love of Christ for them to ponder. We think that these things are a part of the future for the body of Christ, scattered and dispersed, living and active. We are ready and obedient to be used for the new thing God is bringing to pass.

A note on reading this book

The shape of this book mimics the cycles of human community life, lived out in place and in prayer. Prayer is where it begins, in the daily prayer that is both the primary office of every priest of the Church of England and the shared charism of every member of the body of Christ.

Chapters on the other 'occasional offices' – baptism, marriage and funerals – punctuate the rest of the book. They are interspersed between essays that consider 'place' (in a variety of very different settings), 'incarnation' and the Eucharist, and 'study' – the whole-person theology of Christian education.

Part 3 offers a poem on incarnation and mortality (generously allowed to us by the poet Michael Symmons-Roberts), a parish priest's concluding analysis on where we stand and where we face, and some thoughts for the future. Last of all comes a reflection from the former Archbishop, Rowan Williams.

PART I

Place and Priesthood

Office: Daily Prayer

JESSICA MARTIN

South Cambridgeshire

Here the public office of prayer is explored: its ties and over-laps with private intercession and private contemplation; what corporate prayer, corporate living, can mean for the priest pray-ing alone or in a tiny group; what place-rooted prayer can mean in a setting of multiple churches, multiple settlements. Above all the chapter is about praying the time, praying in time, touch-ing past and future; about praying cyclically in a linear world as part of the work of learning to live in the light of eternity.

In the town of West Malling in Kent, in the Anglican Bene-dictine convent every morning the community sings: 'I will bless the Lord at all times.' The words open Psalm 34, and they are the ground of all prayer and all worship. I often hear the community's thin, thready, elderly yet oddly girlish voices in my head as I begin daily prayer in the parishes. I will bless the Lord at all times, good and bad, in loss and in joy. I will always be turned towards praise.

I have a conversation with a curate about the psalms, about the ways in which their vicissitudes seem to speak to her life up to and including her recent ordination, to its pains and inexplic-able griefs. 'And', she says, 'I just hear in my head, over and over, Bless the Lord, Bless the Lord, Bless the Lord. A constant refrain to my day.'

My subject is a particular duty of the parish priest: the duty to pray daily. When priests are ordained, this is one of the

3

promises they make to the bishop. They will observe a rhythm of daily prayer. I am licensed as priest-in-charge of five different churches. I am licensed to pray daily and publicly, and I need to find a way to do this that somehow honours my commitment to all the five churches. It is not immediately obvious how it can be done.

My commitment to pray daily is a public one, offered to the villages I serve, not simply a private understanding between myself and God. The historical roots of daily prayer are explicitly public. Before the Reformation daily prayer in churches followed a monastic pattern of 'offices': prayer several times a day, in the international language, Latin. Prayer in parish churches and in local monastic communities was always public in the sense that it joined the community who prayed with the prayers of Christendom – but it might be unintelligible to locals. After the Reformation the understanding of daily prayer as public was if anything intensified as the content of services was revised so that they might be more intelligible (they were now in English) and more repetitively stable, for those who could not read. But what counted as Christendom had altered for ever, and other alterations in reformed understandings of the more individuated nature of prayer would effect change, slowly, on what people imagined prayer was, and on how they – and therefore I, the inheritor of this history – would perform it and understand it. This tension continues to this day in our shared and differing understandings of what communal prayer is and does.

In descriptive terms what happened to daily public prayer at the Reformation was that it was reduced to a simpler, less variable vernacular form and the number of times it happened per day reduced to two, morning and evening. So from the mid-sixteenth century there has been a formal liturgy in English available for praying in churches morning and evening, and this is expected to be the form of words an Anglican priest will use in daily prayer. Since Anglican priests, unlike those of the free churches, also make a promise at ordination that they will only conduct services in authorized forms, this is a significant point. Daily prayer is public prayer according to an authorized form, and any person who wishes to can attend it. It is to be advertised and it should happen in church.

The basic form authorized for this service today is the same as that devised in the late 1540s by Thomas Cranmer and published as part of the *Book of Common Prayer*, though it has gone through a number of alterations since it first appeared in 1549. Over the last forty years there has been massive liturgical revision seeking a workable modern-language form, and this has settled into the stable and dominant daily prayer of *Common Worship* – itself profoundly influenced by the Anglican Franciscan daily office, a form devised for a vowed religious community. In my churches I use both the *Book of Common Prayer* and *Common Worship*, which in its full daily prayer form has only been available since 2006.

So much for the theory. In practice there is huge variation, depending both on the priest's theological understanding of what they are doing and on what they find personally helpful. 'I can't cope with how *wordy* it all is,' says a colleague despairingly, explaining why she uses a much simpler system. Some, like myself, see what they are doing as a vicarious public office. Others, more reformed, more 'Protestant' and individuated in their understanding, will argue that 'quiet time' spent alone with God in prayer and reading the Bible fulfils their ordination promise just as well if not better than parroting a lot of old words in the same form every day in a cold, empty church. This is not merely a modern phenomenon: there are seventeenth-century complaints that more evangelical vicars do not pray publicly in their churches. Radically different understandings of what daily prayer is and who it is for underpin the two different approaches.

And public prayer is difficult to do. I am not merely talking about personal laziness or disinclination. It is genuinely awkward to make the time without neglecting other duties – to the school, for example, to the local coffee morning, above all

5

to family. It is also a different discipline from private prayer, and a time-poor life can leach away the opportunity for that fundamental activity. When one is very tired private prayer may become sleep almost immediately – but it can become the moment when you realize that you are flooding your body with adrenalin just to keep going on a difficult day. Some time ago, during the Watch of the Passion one Maundy Thursday, I was sitting in the dark listening to the loud drumming of blood in my ears and the banging of my heart, neither of which I could slow throughout the hour I sat there, and realizing that I had been in that state for many, many hours. Now I intermittently take a low-dose beta-blocker – a heart-slower – for those moments when the workload forces my system into overdrive, although I try to manage things so that the medication is not needed. I try to remember regularly to sit before God in silence and only be. Nothing else.

The Morning and Evening Offices are in exactly the same form whether you are praying alone in a church on a Wednesday morning or in a cathedral on Sunday surrounded by your clergy colleagues and a congregation of hundreds. It is still daily prayer. But in practice, during the week, you are quite likely to be praying alone. You might have a few others as regular companions; I pray in company four times a week, but would never expect more than two people there and usually it is only one. So the question of whether this is a private prayer meeting that happens to be in church or a very sparsely populated public office, though clear in theory, never quite goes away in practice. There is a peculiar freedom, as well as loneliness, in the public office offered when alone. But more and more I know that it is not private prayer even if nobody else is there. My discipline of genuinely private prayer – very short, just five minutes morning and evening, with almost no words or structure and with absolutely no petitionary element for myself or anyone else – is something separate from the public offices of prayer which are part of my work as a priest in the places to which I am called.

Every modern Anglican priest with more than one church to care for has to make a decision about whether to pray in each church on a rota basis or to favour one church over another (and on what grounds), and indeed how to manage the routine of daily prayer between different communities. If you have thirteen hamlets, you will not be praying in all of them, and so (you can easily find yourself thinking) why pray in any of them, in the cold and damp and with all the time you spend getting there and back? But if you are committed to daily prayer as a public form then praying in a local church is extremely important.

I also, intermittently, join a local women's prayer group; they commit to meeting regularly before breakfast in someone's home to pray together. Theirs is a tradition of free prayer, personally confiding troubles or concerns or matters for thanksgiving. It is nourishing. It is collaborative. The women who do it are not only sustained by it themselves but offer that sustenance within the parishes in a whole host of different ways. It is private prayer that spills out into our common life as a blessing. My formal prayer is strengthened by their support and wisdom.

In practice I find that I pray most often in the churches in the village where I actually live, and I have a routine that takes in all three churches. But I feel differently about the churches where I pray most frequently, and my relationship with those churches and with those communities is therefore rather different. And – although casual visitors to daily prayer are rare – I *am seen* to do it, expected to pass by clutching my books on the way to the church on Tuesday and Friday mornings just as the retired men come back from the shop with their newspapers and the mums push their younger children home after the school run. And as I go past, people will sometimes ask me to pray for them, or for a relative or friend, and I do.

So, what happens in daily prayer according to these authorized forms? The answer is slightly different for the older and for the newer forms, but they have certain things in common. All have set words that you are expected to say aloud; all assume that these words will be said in a responsorial form (that is to say, a kind of call and answer, where one person leads and the other responds – when you are alone you take both parts). All have readings from the Old and New Testaments on a set daily rota that attempts complete coverage of the Bible within a three-year time-frame. (This rota is shared across the Roman Catholic, Anglican and Anglican Communion churches, as well as the free Protestant churches, so the same passages are read on the same day all over the world.) All daily prayer has responsorial repetition of the psalms, again on a rota – the *Book of Common Prayer*, for example, divides the psalms into thirty chunks, which are then read across Morning and Evening Prayer to make up a recitation of the complete Book of Psalms every calendar month. (*Common Worship* is less ambitious, less comprehensive, and more theme-driven in its selection of psalms to read.)

All daily prayer services have canticles – songs or utterances of song-like construction usually from biblical sources – interspersed with the readings. All daily prayer services contain a petitionary element, a penitential element, a praise element, and a Collect (a set prayer summarizing the collective prayer of those present, and changing weekly). All daily prayer services say the Lord's Prayer, the form of words Jesus gives his disciples in the Gospels when they ask how they should pray. And all daily prayer services, as today's Anglican priests do them, have a free space into which local needs, sorrows, events and difficulties are spoken – though in the older BCP service the permission to do this is not explicit.

So far, so uniform. But there are differences too. On the days of the week when I pray according to the older form of the *Book of Common Prayer*, I am required to say at least one prayer for the monarch. These have vanished from the modern form, which behaves implicitly more like the prayer of a disestablished public institution. I approach the discipline of praying for the constitutional monarchy as a way of praying for the country's governance and for its adhesion to just principles, without having to name or endorse any particular government and its vagaries of policy. I treat the monarch as the kind of symbolic figure I myself am being when I pray on behalf of a community many of whom may neither know nor care that this is my duty and my habit.

The other really significant difference between the *Book of Common Prayer* and *Common Worship* is that the newer form is much harder to use and much less mnemonic. *Common Worship* has seasonal variations according to where we are in the church year – Christmas, Lent, Easter, and so on – which necessitate changing large swathes of the set prayers and forms to suit the theme for the season. This involves a lot of flicking backwards and forwards, and it's no accident that the book comes equipped with a mass of coloured fabric markers. It takes for granted the literacy of its users; and the proliferation of forms of text means that even the highly literate unpractised person who happens along is bound to get lost. By the same token it is a form that devalues repetition and is wholly uninterested in the phenomenon of learning prayers by heart. It is, on the other hand, more engaged than the BCP in joining linear and liturgical time because of its insistence on observing the seasons of the church year. It is in form closer to the complex monastic office books ditched at the Reformation, but with an overlay of modern perceptions of text as swift, profuse, protean, variable and expendable. The online daily postings, which lay out the right forms for each day of the year, are well used (when I worked as an academic I would try to start the working day with daily prayer on the computer in my teaching room). There are also handy apps for phones, which most busy parish priests have recourse to, although I try not to (my phone can be a locus of anxiety, not of prayer) unless driven to it by pressure of time.

While these are important differences there is, nevertheless, much similarity in the two forms of daily prayer. And the really important thing about both of them is that they bring together a variety of understandings of time, and they perform that juxtaposition in a context that sees each of those temporal forms in the light of eternity – in the presence of God.

By 'time' I mean three things: first, history or narrative event; second, experience or feeling; and last, duration. These three understandings mingle in daily prayer so subtly that it is difficult to distinguish and draw them out, so all I can do here is describe them, and it will be the reader's task to work out which you think is which.

So: I come into a building that stands on Saxon foundations and has been the location for public prayer since that time. As I walk across the threshold I tread upon the medieval grave of one of my predecessors, a forgotten priest of the village of Hinxton, buried across the opening to his church's porch. I kneel in the chancel, alone or with a companion or two. If I am with a companion we will probably talk for a while, settling what we are doing in the context of who's ill, who's getting married, who's had a baby, who has died, who is in trouble, who are quarrelling, and how we ourselves are feeling just then. Kneeling marks the point of silence, after which there will be no informality. We bring our neighbours and their current preoccupations into the church along with us in our talk, and then we lay them down in order to turn into the presence of God. We speak a shared invocation, which has elements repeated day by day so that quickly no book becomes necessary.

Then we say the day's psalms, taking turns, a verse each. Saying the psalms has been central to Christian daily prayer since the second century and probably earlier. They have, of course, been a part of Jewish prayer ritual for much, much longer than that. Some psalms are narrative, but relatively few. Most express first-person experience, often elliptically, with buried fragmentary narratives of situations one can only guess at, human joy and praise and suffering and arrogance and anger and fear and despair and trust, addressed to God in disjunctive chunks of feeling. I inhabit the 'I', the first-person perspective of a variety of human longings some of which I do not personally know. I have never been afraid for my life in the face of a great army. I have never been a refugee or an exile. I have never been a king, or a beggar, or a complete social outcast. I have never even been so consumed with the longing for the presence of God that it has deprived me of a single night's sleep. I have never wished an enemy dead, or cursed his children. I do not yet know terminal illness, or old age. I am performing and uttering a depth and a height of human desire that I can recognize but it is only mine insofar as I am joined to the universal human family where such experience becomes common. Without saying the psalms I would be deaf and blind to the range of human longing in God's presence and diminished in my own sense of what that is.

There are quite a variety of theological perspectives on what work the psalms do in prayer, and what I have described is probably closer to Bonhoeffer's view than the classic position that the psalms represent the human 'I' of Christ's incarnational perspective; I can only describe what happens to me. They are poetry, and as poetry they swing back and forth between meaning something deeply personal and speaking something deeply alien. They are also at times typological; particular psalms speak to particular points in the Christian narrative analogically. No Christian can read the Passion psalm, Psalm 22, which begins with the words Jesus utters from the cross, 'My God, my God, why hast thou forsaken me,' without reading that particular moment of despair into every following line. And Psalm 103, spoken at my wedding twenty years ago, is also the psalm I will speak at every funeral committal:

Like as a father pitieth his own children: even so is the Lord merciful unto them that fear him.
For he knoweth whereof we are made: he remembereth that we are but dust.
The days of man are but as grass: for he flourisheth as a flower of the field.
For as soon as the wind goeth over it, it is gone: and the place thereof shall know it no more.

But the merciful goodness of the Lord endureth for ever and ever upon them that fear him: and his righteousness upon children's children.

I wonder about the nature of that mercy, placed in such a context, in the mortality of every living soul which nevertheless finds sustenance in the enduring presence of God. This is comfort that has nothing to do with human immortality – quite the reverse – but empties the greedy desires of the self to contemplate the enduring nature of a goodness that lives behind and before the brief flowering and human forgetting of each individual life. I didn't think much about it at thirty, in my wedding dress; but at forty and onwards it suddenly made sense, became genuine comfort.

Canticles and readings follow the psalms. Canticles are fixed points, and they join together local time with sacred time. For example, the canticle for Morning Prayer, the Benedictus, is a lightly versified form of the prayer uttered by John the Baptist's father in the Gospel of Luke, which prophesies his new baby John to be herald of the Messiah and the coming of Jesus as a new sign of hope, just as the morning star promises the coming of day. The reason we say it every morning is partly to proclaim our own local, immediate new day as a new beginning, the first hour of the transformed rest of your life in God's sight, and partly to recall and re-impress the nature of God's promise as the covenantal framework for that daily transformation. 'Blessed be the Lord ... for he hath visited, and redeemed his people ... the day-spring from on high hath visited us; to give light to them that sit in darkness, and in the shadow of death: and to guide our feet into the way of peace.' I can never say those last words without seeing in my mind's eye those in my parishes who are dying. And, since I live in a retirement demographic, my parishioners are dying every week.

A quick word about repetition. Doing something daily with the same structure in the same words has a peculiar effect. It's as if you are laying down layers each day that exist not in linear time but on top of each other, making a patina or artefact that belongs outside time altogether. For example: from my first week in the parishes for four years I said Evening Prayer on a Friday with one particular parishioner, Tom, who had terminal cancer – we prayed together every week, while he got iller and iller. I pray today with another companion for whom, in the midst of constant difficulties, the space of daily prayer is a safe space to weep. We pray without Tom, of course, since his body is ashes now, but I can hear his voice with its Sheffield accent speaking the psalms with us; it seems to be happening independently of any of us, in some indescribable elsewhere.

Take an evening canticle, the Song of Mary, still called the Magnificat after its pre-Reformation Latin opening. This song of triumph is the pregnant Mary's reworking of a song by her Old Testament precursor, Hannah. Hannah, who lived in a corrupt and greedy society, who longed for a baby and whose desperate prayer was heard by God when she prayed in a semi-abandoned, badly run Temple, sees in the new life she carries in her body a miraculous reversal in the power structures of the world, where the poor and the dispossessed and the hungry are given all that they lack and the rich are sent empty away. Mary sings Hannah, and I sing Mary. 'All generations shall call me blessed,' we say together, and because I speak Mary's words they become performative. Three kinds of now – Hannah's joy at the baby she longed for, Mary's at the baby she never looked for, and the contingent now of the present moment – exist for a thick instant, together. I said the Magnificat through my own late gift of pregnancy, and through the years of longing and trying for another child, and now into the outskirts of menopause, in a world where the rich get richer and the poor get poorer and our affluent nation – even in my own comfortable villages – contains more and more hungry children, more and more families in debt.

The canticles are bolstered on each side by Bible readings, from the Old and the New Testaments successively. These are, of course, as extraordinarily various as the Bible itself – it might be the narratives of a nation's self-understanding, the fierce rules of a beleaguered tiny society, the stories and recollections of Jesus' acts and words, the working out of the structures and self-understanding of the early Christian Church, poetry, prose, lamentation, warning, promise. The juxtapositions are often jarring, sometimes serendipitous. You are participating in a kind of temporal collage, with yourself and your experience as conduit, not as centre. If you have a place, it is often one rather like those fifteenth-century Flemish paintings, where the donor kneels at the side and contemplates the action of which she is not a part but is a witness.

Last of all, at the end of the formal recitation of the structures of public prayer, comes the bit most people recognize as 'prayer' in the modern sense of personal petition. This is for me a funny mixture of intercession and a kind of marking of the flowerings and depredations of time in the eye of eternity. I don't *ask* for much, beyond the presence of God in various circumstances – the covenant promise, 'I am with you', tugged on, reminding God or perhaps just reminding myself. I name the sick and commend them into God's hand; name the recently dead and pray for their families. We have a long list, updated every month, of those who have asked for prayer, a tiny proportion of whom will be churchgoers. We name the new babies and those preparing for baptism, the wedding couples, the troubles and concerns of the wider world.

Why do it? My answer might be very different from that of those who ask for prayer. On the way back from the school run one morning, one of the mothers asked me to pray for her stepdad because he had had a surprise diagnosis of terminal pancreatic cancer. I went down to the church and said Morning Prayer with a retired priest colleague, and there was a man already there, sitting with a bag and a newspaper, a man I didn't know. Among those we prayed for I named this woman's stepdad. You will have guessed that the man in church was the person I had named – and mightily surprised he was, since he didn't live in the village, had never met me, and had only had the diagnosis for a matter of days. However, I then had quite a tricky conversation with him; it seemed that he viewed being named in church as a kind of automatic or even miraculous healing act, and he appeared to see his past divorce as a kind of moral reason for the coming of his cancer. He died about six months later. These are not my views of what I do when I pray for the sick, or my diagnosis of the random acts of malign nature; my job is to be a kind of faulty join between human need and the goodness of God, and I feel deeply my limitations of love to manage anything better than that. But this man's view is not universal by any means; when the husband of a terminally ill woman asks for prayer for her it is not because he thinks prayer will stop her dying, but because (I think) her public naming joins her in with the living in an act of love, and this is an effort she is no longer able to make for herself. He sits with her, seemingly isolated, but when her name goes on the list and is spoken in church they are held in a kind of symbolic community.

One final thing. The discipline of daily prayer convinces me that I am not an individual. My physical separateness is a misleading distraction from the truth that everything about me, from the patterning I received from my parents to make this separate body to the multitude of influences that have shaped my perceptions, is bound up in the rest of the human family of which I am only a part. My past, including the irrecoverable bits, my own dead forebears, the demolished buildings at which I was schooled, has a constant presence that is nothing to do with me or with human memory, a constant juxtaposing now which I can glimpse in a fragmentary way in the different forms of time crushed clumsily together in the daily offices of Morning and Evening Prayer. One practitioner, George Guiver, describes the practice of prayer as 'the great company of voices'. I do not worry that when my own voice can no longer speak there may be nothing but silence. There are always other voices.

The Priest Attends Seven Village Fetes: Multi-Parish Ministry[1]

CHERYL COLLINS AND JESSICA MARTIN

Rural Suffolk and South Cambridgeshire

In this chapter, two priests-in-charge of multi-parish benefices converse. Some of the fractured and plural nature of such ministry is reflected in the double voice of the conversation itself: not a linear reflection, but a multiple one, backwards and forwards between temporary points of rest, before moving again to another approach. The conversation focuses on four themes: Presence, Example, Memory and Refreshment.

Presence

Cheryl: Three of my parishes have planned their Harvest Suppers for the same evening. I am not entirely surprised that in this 'united benefice' they haven't consulted one another. It leaves me with a delicate, but familiar problem: which parish shall I honour with my presence? Some of my predecessors dealt with the situation by completely avoiding both PCCs and parish social/fundraising events.[2] But I cannot do that. It offends both my understanding of the importance of 'being

---

1 The title comes courtesy of a colleague in one of St Edmundsbury and Ipswich's Deanery Chapters who plaintively wondered how one could cope with this, especially when several parishes schedule them for the same day.

2 It seems only fair to mention that at the time this six-parish benefice post was half-stipend (I'll not insult them by calling it half-time).

with' my parishioners as a symbolic reminder of God's unseen presence, and my experience of ministry, which reminds me that social events present surprising pastoral opportunities. So what should be my criteria for choice? Do I stick with the parish that got it in my diary first? Do I choose the smallest village and most struggling congregation and therefore perhaps the one most in need of support? Or do I choose the parish that is fundraising after a recent lead theft as a gesture of my solidarity in their trouble?

Jessica: The 'fairness' principle is a very tricky judgement call. There's an expectation that the multi-benefice minister will share her presence out as equally as possible – regardless of size, vitality, population, proportion of share paid, and so on. But fairness has its problems. For example, it's eminently fair for our three churches to share out the 10 a.m. parish communion between them across the month (and similarly with the early and the evening services, which also rotate). But it makes the monthly pattern complex to understand and this deters casual visitors. My husband still doesn't know it – after six years! – and asks me every week what church we are in. It doesn't invite or support growth, and it makes churchgoing the *difficult* choice; rather like a rural bus-user, you have to know the vagaries of the timetable before you start. At which point anyone who's got a car abandons the buses even if parking will be a nightmare when they get there. I'd like to move to a pattern where each church offers something (not necessarily the same something, not necessarily a communion, not necessarily clergy-led) at the same time-slot every week, so that everyone locally knows that there will be church at 9.30 a.m. every week no matter what Sunday it is in the month. But to do that is no longer to share the prime worship time (or the priest) equally. Who should get it? Should it be the church that struggles most, or the one that already has some vitality upon which to build? At what point does shoring up weakness mean spending all your time on artificial respiration, at the expense of good initiatives? The luxury of three parishes (a very small multi-benefice unit) makes it possible to project a regular pattern; but what happens when you have five, seven, ten, fifteen? What can be sustained or predictable in such a setting?

Cheryl: Yes, an ongoing point of contention and drama in any multi-parish benefice is the worship rota. This complex map of who is having what service when and who will be leading that service can be charged with all sorts of underlying messages about power, expectations, and the complicated horse-trading necessary to arrive at something to which all can give some kind of assent. For most multi-parish set-ups it is impossible to provide a service in each place each week, even at wildly varying times. Many smaller villages lost a weekly service years ago, and at least some members of the congregation have no desire for more. While the 'core' congregation may include those who are happy to travel round the benefice, for the penumbra the complexity of the rota can be an excuse not to go; and those who move here from a committed churchgoing background may prefer driving into town, as they do for other things, to join a congregation with a predictable weekly pattern. Clergy often find that it is the lure of the 'special' that will bring people to church, with little interest shown in making a regular commitment.

Jessica: The heavily publicized 'special' event for a particular group (usually but not exclusively young families) is certainly one way I have tried to make a virtue of necessity. I think many rural parish priests tackle the problem of being spread thinly by giving up on predictability and trying instead for visibility, for (frankly) affinity marketing on the occasional event that will stand out. The occasions are designed, of course, to join up with each other in order to develop a worshipping community with something already in common who will look forward to coming together. They do work. I think it's interesting that Fresh Expressions groups are taking off in rural areas. But it has dangers too: if 'specialness' has become ordinary currency it delays that moment of realization in the churchgoer that they need to make a quotidian commitment – with their presence and personal gifts (including financial commitment). At the same time, working to create like-minded worshipping communities of the same sort of person (the elderly, the bereaved, the parent/child) can have divisive effects on the church family itself, because people start to have consumerist expectations of bespoke, separate ministry and worship for separate interest groups and don't see the virtues of coming together or making allowances for each other's spiritual needs. I think it's important to bear in mind that affinity marketing divides as it builds.

But, having said all that, gathering interest groups for worship and study does have a real value of its own: it provides an emotionally comfortable forum for people to grow in faith and confidence, and it turns the fact of the multiple benefice from a problem to a kind of advantage, though one that echoes the fragmented community of secular support groups (*Slimming World* or whatever[3]) more than I quite like. Still, it works, and that's important.

Cheryl: Yes, because it's what we've got. A recent book on multi-congregation ministry[4] quoted the statistic that in 2011 71 per cent of Church of England parishes were in multi-congregational amalgamations of one kind or another. Certainly in a semi-rural diocese like St Edmundsbury and Ipswich, only six of the eighteen deaneries have single-parish benefices, and

---

3 The French sociologist Danièle Hervieu-Léger, invoking the work of Gilles Lipovetsky, considers the 'relational craze' in modern society (i.e. the proliferation of support groups for particular, often extreme, personal situations) to be a result of the rise of the same fragmented individualism that threatens religious stability, offering 'the only antidote to the often unbearable sense of isolation of having to stand on one's own' and as constituting 'an elementary form of ... social recognition of individual meaning' (D. Hervieu-Leger, *Religion as a Chain of Memory*, tr. Simon Lee (Cambridge: Polity Press, 2000), pp. 94–5). Which suggests that religious identity may also be forged through like-minded interest groups.

4 Malcolm Grundy, *Multi-congregation Ministry* (London: Canterbury Press, 2015), p. 1.

these are in the population centres. Even in these places, there are multi-parish groupings and a fear that more will shortly follow as the number of stipendiary clergy continues to decline. That's one of the problems, of course: these groupings do not exist because of a positive strategy but as a reaction to the fact that there are not enough priests to go round. While it's a myth to believe that there ever were, there has been dramatic change. In 1960 only 17 per cent of churches were in amalgamations.[5] It is not surprising that parishioners imagine how wonderful it was when they had the vicar 'all to themselves', and clergy torture themselves with the impossibility of being fully present in six places at once.

Jessica: That is the dilemma. Parish amalgamations do not unite, but shove together a set of single units, each of which is constructed assuming the constant presence of a dedicated parish priest. The parish year has a pattern based upon that constant presence – he or she will be expected to be familiar in the school, at the shops, walking the dog, at meetings of locally based charities, at community events whether or not they are connected directly with the church: summer fetes, civic commemorative gatherings, and so on. In this sense regularity and predictability are everything, casual encounter is expected, intimate local knowledge is presumed. Multiply that by six and the community depth of the model is fatally weakened and its accessibility and predictability swamped. Add the fact that many villages have lost their other community markers – post offices, schools, shops – and the context for the old model is not there either. All this creates that strange paradoxical sense that while hardly anyone seems actually to attend worship, the days are filled with local demands; the traditionally focused priest will be busy doing a whole bunch of community things, which are the village's baseline expectations but which don't

---

5 *From Anecdote to Evidence: Findings from the Church Growth Research Programme 2011–2013*, www.churchgrowthresearch.org.uk, p. 28.

and won't fill the church. But if you don't do them you will never know your people – and it is through relationships that rural churches grow.

Cheryl: Community involvement has lots of virtues. In my six parishes the congregation is still largely rooted (at least in the short term), not gathered from a wider area, and the church and congregation have at least some sense of being connected to and existing for the wider community. Pastoral care often remains local, and wherever possible people here still expect to come and 'pay their respects' to other members of the community at their funerals. So there's a context in a wider community and an opportunity for pastoral care that does not result in purely instrumental relationships. And those are reasons why rural ministry can feel like I'm most truly exercising the ministry I'm called to. However, less attractive is the administrative overwhelm, when everything is duplicated six times, not to mention the disjunction between my optimistic belief that I'm ministering to a group of parishes and the belief of my parishioners that they are merely sharing a vicar. When working largely alone it can certainly seem as if everything goes worse when it is multiplied by three, six, or more. So the situation of multi-parish benefices can feel like the most intense microcosm of all that besets the Church at present.

Jessica: I thought about this when I arrived in the villages I serve, which are not far from population centres: a short drive from both Cambridge and Saffron Walden. So villagers can get bespoke high-quality worship of every possible variety just by driving a short distance – and they drive for everything else, so why not this? The people who will stick with the village church will be those who value the local, whether electively or as a matter of deep identity.

Marilyn Strathern's famous anthropological study of the village of Elmdon looks at its kinship and community patterns. Elmdon is about five miles from my southernmost village,

Ickleton (though the diocesan boundary parts them) and the two both warred with each other and intermarried with each other. The study is set in the early 1960s but has a postscript dated 1977. Reading her book, I recognized an awful lot about the community described, but mostly in historic terms – the centrality and authority of the church presence, the fixed population, centred on agricultural labour for local gentlemen farmers, the complex web of family relationships binding most residents. But already there were 'incomers' buying and repairing the pretty but primitive and tumbledown houses, putting bathrooms and heating in while the 'old villagers' went into the newly built council houses that at the time were so much more comfortable. There were tensions and complaints about the way the 'incomers' were taking charge of community activities and reshaping them according to their visions of what a village idyll should contain. Nowadays that process is more or less complete, so that community identity is largely contributed to by incomers with a strong civic sense of what a village should be. They are regarded with scepticism, affection, friendliness, amusement or irritation by the few remaining 'old villagers', according to temperament. Some members of the old families are still centrally placed but many are elderly and living in outlying social housing bungalows or almshouses funded directly or indirectly by church and village historic charities. Their children and grandchildren have been priced out. And each of the villages contains a largish minority for whom the village is simply a dormitory, however much they may have bought their property on a fantasy of community living.

Although the church no longer commands authority of the kind Strathern and her team observed (the chancel liability debacle of 2013 exposed the extent to which village churches simply cannot afford to *demand* anything at all, though *asking* can bring in an extraordinarily generous response), it nevertheless thrives more in those villages that have preserved some collective sense of community responsibility. In larger villages the community identity of the church is quite circumscribed, and Remembrance Sunday and possibly the midnight service at Christmas are the only occasions that seem fundamental to the wider village's sense of itself. In smaller villages the church has a symbolic central role that is much easier to build upon, and (not coincidentally) the village itself has a much stronger collective sense of its own history and ongoing identity. In my most challenged (and largest) village there is a fragmented sense of nostalgia for a lost past and rather more anxious digging for its narrative – the local 'Duxford Revisited' slide shows command a wide audience – and *all* the community organizations, including the school, complain about apathy. I can't say definitively, in the end, why that village is so adrift from its church community, but I do think the 'village temper' has something to do with it; also history (and especially perhaps the history of my predecessors' relationships, and indeed the history of nonconformism there) has an awful lot to contribute – going back a long way, not just a generation or two. Presence matters.

Example

Cheryl: Of course, you could say that George Herbert had a multi-parish benefice in Bemerton with Fugglestone St Peter, but he was also blessed with two curates!

We have talked before about the way in which Herbert, a figure we have both studied, was a kind of silent or underlying partner in how we understand our ministry. Much of our conversation has reflected issues that occupy the wider Church: finance, buildings, the need for simplification, the effect of the physical presence or otherwise of the priest, how to maintain complex patterns of communal worship and should these be sacramental or not, how does the congregation relate to the wider community, what can we reasonably expect of the laity.[6] Not Herbertian problems! I'd add to Herbert's

---

6 Indeed, these also appear in the recent report *Released for Mission: Growing the Rural Church*, GS Misc. 1092.

influential example the more modern figure of Alan Ecclestone in his ministry at Darnell. The ministries of both Herbert and Ecclestone were made up of clearly defined tasks: study and sermon preparation, catechizing, visiting, hospitality. Modern administrative burdens, and the meetings that go with a thinly stretched institution, add to those tasks for today's rural priest. It can sometimes feel as if the vital connections between study, visiting, preaching, praying and occasional offices are being diluted or even lost.

For Herbert, this was all part of a model of incarnational presence, about living in one place and not another. When you are physically shared between a number of places the ministerial weight shifts to a kind of vicarious model, where because you aren't present but find ways to make physical connections in the villages, other people aren't present in the churches but find ways to be connected through you. So people in my parishes like to have some kind of relationship with the priest as the official representative holy person, and to give me their anxieties so that I can carry them and take them to church. Perhaps they feel that it saves them having to do so or that I have the necessary skills for such a task and they do not.

Herbert does, of course, draw on more ancient models of ministry in his work, and presents a kind of ideal that may never have existed (as Justin Lewis-Anthony points out in his book *If You Meet George Herbert on the Road, Kill Him*). It's almost as if the understanding of monastic life which saw it as upholding the rest of life through prayer has been replaced by another kind of 'professional Christian' who operates on behalf of the wider Christian community and upholds standards that others (despite the proliferation after the Reformation of books on household piety) can never be expected to achieve.

Jessica: I think there's a strong relationship between faith and need. That sounds (and is) obvious but it has huge implications. Herbert lived and worked in a culture which assumed, on the whole, that people needed God, and in which the frailty of being human, and the realities of death, disease and scarcity were constantly visible. The same was true, differently, of Ecclestone. Each of those men had a part to play in meeting community need and behind them was a receding vista of examples and models of holy living that could be leaned on, admired and imitated. The past was constantly being remade in the vitality of the present (sometimes in situations of acute cultural flux that make modernity look like a stroll in the park). Modern culture talks a lot about the need for role models, but our media is particularly focused on showing us that heroes have feet of clay, even as it also peddles the idea that no one really needs to be penitent (or forgiven) for anything they do. And forgetting rather than transforming the past is one of the necessary penalties of self-actualization – whether it's forgetting the life you led with your last wife/husband or the life you led when you were poorer or sadder before you made good, or the desperately poor agricultural roots of your nice chocolate-box village, or whatever.

So today's priests, especially perhaps among the affluent, are in a rather odd position: few people will say that they have any need either of them or of God; few people will recognize that parish priests have a role to play in helping people change their lives, live with their frailties and mistakes, make flourishing relationships with God and with each other. Few people will even accept that they *are* frail, either morally or physically, until circumstances force them into it. (I find myself thinking sometimes about the end of Shaw's play about the Sally Army, *Major Barbara*, where Barbara notices that the comfortable are in the worst mess of all.) So – it's all perfect, nothing for the priest to do. Only – people and things do go wrong, sometimes through wrongdoing, selfishness and evil, and sometimes through accident and circumstance. Everyone has heartbreak, everyone is mortal. There does need to be some coherent vision of collective goodness that is larger than the sum of its parts. And priests are still allowed in a kind of tacit way to inhabit, or visit, the needy empty space in people's lives which used to have God in it. As long as they don't bang on about it too much.

So I pray a good deal for people who ask for it. But they don't come to spend time with me while I pray. Maybe that's because I can't come often enough to spend time with them – though I try.

Memory

Cheryl: Jessica speaks elsewhere in this volume about the church and churchyard as material versions of memory palaces. The importance of this cannot be overstated. Our memories make us who we are. Remembering is an important part of grief, but when we remember our dead we also remember who shaped us and how we have been shaped. We honour our own identities as they have been given to us.

All Souls services are one moment when the church connects with the wider community by acknowledging this need to remember and honour. When the rest of the world has forgotten our loss the church says, 'We remember, and we count every person valuable and worth remembering because they are children of God, remembered by God.' When you send out the invitations to the annual All Souls service it is dangerous to make assumptions about who will or will not come. For everyone has a need to hear their loved one named before God, to light a candle to remember, light from light, how their own identity has been shaped by the one they remember.

Jessica: The sociologist Danièle Hervieu-Léger has written about how memory works in relation to religious belief. She's writing about France, and the book is twenty years old now, but I find its theory of memory maps compellingly onto what I find in the English village context. She says that religion flourishes most easily in places with a stable tradition and a shared history which confers settled identities onto its adherents, and that once people put their individual good above collective goods – either family or community – then religion declines because its shared world-view suffers and people instead make up a bits-and-bobs spirituality of their own to suit them. (They usually go on believing something supernatural, but they exit from shared tradition.) The casualty of all this, she says, is shared, locally based cultural memory – at which point people begin to seek it in fragmented ways in order to understand who they are. This is when 'accelerated change, which is at the root of the characteristic instantaneousness of both individual and collective memory, paradoxically gives rise to appeals to memory. They underpin the need to recover the past in the imagination without which collective memory, just as individual identity, is unable to operate.' In villages like mine you have constant genealogical inquiries from people scattered all over the world, a strong, almost anxious interest in the local history of the last hundred years, and a very strong response both to the life-histories of the recently dead and to the 'Remembrance' traditions of both World Wars. In all these things the church is understood and assumed to be central.

Cheryl: There are striking parallels, yes. The introduction of an All Souls service in my own benefice was something I brought with me, but the impetus to remember and honour those who died in the First World War and to mark the centenary of the beginning of this conflict came entirely from the community. I had waited to see if there was any interest in doing something and then one parish decided they wanted to hold a vigil on 4 August 2014. I worked with them to put together a mixture of poetry and prayers and we listened together to *Fantasia on a Theme of Thomas Tallis*, which struck the note of being about home without being overly martial. Although it wasn't widely advertised we had all sorts of people we don't normally see in church turning up. They thought that church was the place to go for this corporate remembering, and they brought their children with them because they felt it was important to pass on the memory. Later, on Remembrance Sunday, we gathered together the work that local people had done in finding out the history behind some of the names on our memorials and we read all these out. Who their parents were, what job they had done in secular life, where they died. Not only did we get many people from the present village communities but relatives of some of the dead men came back to the villages to remember and affirm their own family identities. Relationships and the way they shape our identities are so important.

Refreshment

Cheryl: I've just written up the result of conversations with eleven of the deanery chapters in my diocese. There were grievances and frustrations, of course, but the overwhelming sense of what I received from these conversations was a sense of yearning.

'The well is deep,' says Herbert, 'and we have nothing of our own to draw with.' The yearning I identified in my colleagues, and which I experience myself, is a yearning for relationship, for connection, with God above all.

Too often, in our anxiety, we decide to skip the theology and get straight on with brainstorming the solutions to our problems as a church. We try and answer questions about what we should be doing without fully reflecting on what we are called to be. (When I say 'we' I refer both to the whole Church of God and to the ordained portion of it, because questions of ecclesiology and ministry are hopelessly tangled.)

Jessica: Yes – but the 'hopeless tangle' of ministry and ecclesiology is incredibly important in the multi-parish context! When there are not enough priests to go round, lay incarnational presence is absolutely vital.

Cheryl: But – we tend to leap straight to the questions of church and ministry that are obsessing us, rather than taking time to focus upon God and let God set our agendas. This is a function of communal and individual anxieties as much as anything else, but when I reflect on it I get the feeling that we are more like the priests of Baal, anxiously trying technique after technique, than like Elijah.

The way that the story of Elijah continues after his encounter with the priests of Baal also provides food for thought for the busy multi-parish priest. We can identify with feeling so overwhelmed and so desperately lonely that, like Elijah, we might long to lie down under the broom bush ready to die. But the story reminds us that the one who calls us is faithful. Like Elijah, we may find that hearing God's word in our situation requires the kind of intense listening that can pick out a still small voice, or hear God in the sound of silence. And far from being alone we can discover that we are part of something much larger, even if not quite the 7,000 who had not bowed the knee to Baal.

For us as Christians this can only mean putting aside anxiety, moving the focus from the Church and how we are trying to fix it and onto God. We are asking, 'What is God doing in our world and in our neighbourhoods/villages/towns?' This approach invites us to focus upon the agency of God before thinking about how the church should respond. The shape and character of the church should be determined by our response to what God is doing, reflected in the life of God where we are.

This is the preoccupation of a number of American and English theological practitioners from a range of backgrounds. They are moving towards a kind of 'deep incarnation', which roots the church (here best understood as people rather than building or institution) firmly within the neighbourhood it inhabits, and invites listening as 'perhaps the greatest demonstration that you do not conceive of yourself as God'.[7] What are we listening for? Where and how is God at work here? The new parish is conceived as 'all relationships where the local church

7 Paul Sparks, Tim Soerens and Dwight J. Friesen, *The New Parish* (Downers Grove, IL: IVP, 2014).

lives out its faith together'. The church together functions as a kind of cultural pedagogy of formation, where through the practices of the Christian pilgrimage (presence, listening, discernment, reflection, as worked out in the rich treasure chest of Christian spirituality in such things as Bible study, prayer in all its forms, the sacraments and so on) we continue to grow into our identity as children of God and bring the fruits of that identity as gifts to the wider community. So, for instance, to questions of economy we bring our understanding of God's abundance and our thanksgiving, to questions of environment we offer the perspective of stewardship, to education we bring our broad understanding of formation, and to the civic life we bring the spiritual disciplines of listening, bridge-building and discernment. Part of the wisdom required is to ask what is truly core to our Christian identity and what is merely habitual or customary. This practice of faithful presence also requires us to surrender our illusion that we can control agendas and relationships. It invites us to see worship as the whole of our lives being placed before God as an offering so that within our local community we can be the body of Christ.

Although on one level this might sound very different from the reality of local churches, the focus upon faithful presence fits the charism of the Anglican Church well and chimes in with the kind of faithful pastoral ministry that many clergy speak of as being one of the joys and privileges of parish ministry. This is about 'loving the un-loveable', 'making God real', or maybe better put as pointing to the reality of God already present. The challenge is for this to become something that is understood as the gift of the whole church, not just the ordained.

Jessica: It's back to the 'vicarious vicar' again, isn't it? If you are seen as the person who has the job to pray, the 'prayer professional', how can the community pray together? It takes a disaster to bring that about – a murder or a terrible local accident. In ordinary circumstances sacred and secular are seen as very distinct spheres and there are few places where they meet easily. I hope that the initiative to bring churches back into community use – as post offices and so on – will blur the distinction again, because until we see churches as part of the common good the lasting local relationships we make will find it much harder to skip the barrier. It's not only that *we* are finding it difficult to get God out of church. Other people find it difficult to see God working out of church too.

Cheryl: We can do something, though. It's not that people aren't being the body of Christ in the way they care for grandchildren, shop for an elderly neighbour, seek to build community identity through the thankless task of organizing the village fete. But we've not always been good at naming them as part of our worship, valuing them and upholding one another in prayer in them. One practical approach to facilitating such a cultural change is talked about in the book *Imagine Church: Releasing Whole-life Disciples* by Neil Hudson. Are we in fact equipping the whole Church of God for the wrong thing, prioritizing preparing them for roles in leading in church worship rather than worshipping in the rest of their lives?

When I looked carefully in my own neighbourhood I found signs of God's presence as well as the issues and frustrations so often rehearsed. They seem like small oases in the desert of our predicament. They invite us to try and work out not how we can prop up our struggling structures but how to respond to God's presence here. Just as the prophetic poets of exile spoke God's reality into the despair of those still clinging to old paradigms and failed structures, so one task of ordained ministry today might be as water diviners, discerning and naming where God's living water is springing up in our midst. These moments of epiphany, explicit or implicit, are often generated by the community as a whole or by people who have not dared to consider and name what they are doing as ministry.

Jessica: I do see that, but the reason we are here at all is because someone has decided to fund ministry in the places where we are. Fresh from the (receding) threat that I might be required to stretch myself solely over five or perhaps seven churches (at which point I wouldn't be able to do more than manage decline), I find myself nagging away at how our structures might support rural ministry better. I am parochially minded, and instinctively committed to the parish system; but I don't see how the 'coverage' model is going to work unless we alter the relationships between lay and ordained ministry very radically indeed.

Cheryl: The direction of my own quotidian thoughts has been affirmed by reading *A Nazareth Manifesto* by Sam Wells. Wells contends that the most accurate way to describe the very heart of God and the nature of God's purpose and destiny for us is not 'for' but 'with'. We see the 'with' at the heart of God in the perichoretic dance of the Trinity and we experience that 'with' pitching a tent among us in the incarnation. He understands the crux of the gospel as being reconciliation, bringing in to right relationship, relationship that forms a solid foundation for all our other relationships and helps us to discover ourselves as communities of abundant flourishing, not scarcity and barrenness. This changes the narrative of the multi-parish benefice altogether.

So what are these signs of hope? Actually, one is in the way people ask me to pray. It takes me to the centre of my priestly identity even if that's also a lonelier place than it could be if we were praying together. Priests are called to pray, to be with God with the people on our heart. It's interesting to me that this is what people generally ask me to do – not the thousand and one tasks the institutional church asks me to do, but the people of my parishes. They know that this is my job, this is who I am. They assume the relationship I have with God, and ask me to mention their concern next time I'm having a chat.

Another small sign of God's presence is regularly incarnated in our local farm shop and café. It's the only shop within the six parishes and apart from the pubs the only place where people can regularly meet and share food and drink together. I started a knit and natter group, by which I mean that I advertised the fact that I would be knitting and nattering there every Thursday morning. The group itself has become a thriving expression of relationship, of mutual love, concern and support. It's a place where the chronically ill (and therefore not at work), the bereaved, the lonely can find a home. Like walking my dog, the everyday nature of a group of women knitting and nattering makes it a nourishing space. Not only this, but because the farm shop has become a centre of the community, with people constantly dropping in, I can make all sorts of pastoral contact. The congregations of my churches recognize the value of this 'loitering with intent' and support my being there.

Another unexpected place where a spring of water is bubbling up is the reaction of the local community to the problem of lead thefts. One of my churches has lost the entire chancel roof in two separate attacks, and another lost the porch roof twice – they came back and stole the replacement lead. The pub in the village where we lost the chancel roof is – along with the village hall – one of the few other public spaces where people can gather, and the family who run the pub decided to hold a fundraising curry night. This reached those in the community who would probably never come to a fundraiser at church. The atmosphere was one of grace, as the community enjoyed an abundant meal together and gave their support to the church. This is encouragement for the congregation to trust that their neighbours do care and to build relationships and accept the gifts of the wider community.

All this might seem very little: bare trickles of water in a barren landscape. But it is something. It helps us to discern a gift, even in the desert where the challenge is hard to miss. The more I reflect upon it, the more I feel that the practice of water divining, of glimpsing God at work in many different places and people in the communities I serve, gives me moments when I know I am in the right place and doing what I am called to do. With the discernment comes the naming of the gift, so that those who accord me authority in the things of God can begin to discover themselves named as ministers of grace, as embodying the love of God, as the body of Christ together in this place, living out our calling to deep incarnation.

It is not an easily translatable solution to the problems of finance, structures and buildings, but maybe it is what God has given us, and therefore we need to have confidence that through these gentle trickles eventually the desert can blossom and burst into song, though it will be singing a new song.

The Priest Attends a Deathbed: Post-Christian, Multi-Faith Urban Ministry

RICHARD SUDWORTH

Sparkbrook, Birmingham

Richard Sudworth writes of the 'pared-down' blessings of his marginal context, where the largely first-generation Afro-Caribbean Christians of his congregation are now hugely outnumbered by citizens of other faiths. He considers the Christian promise of resurrection in the context of different kinds of death and dying: institutional, personal, congregational. Last, he notices the generous role from time to time granted to the local Anglican church by multi-faith communities seeking a hospitable space for speaking with one, civic voice.

July 2007 was a notable month for Sparkbrook: it held the day a tornado ripped through inner-city Birmingham, tearing up trees and shredding roofs as it snaked along the Victorian terraces. I remember it vividly as I was in the top floor of a local mosque talking to the imam. He had just been interrupted on his mobile phone, the James Bond theme music of his ring-tone puncturing our small voices in the echoing chamber of the mosque's dome. We could feel a sudden change in temperature, clouds darkening through the windows of the mosque, and then a huge thud as the fire doors burst open. It was over in seconds but the trail of damage it left was significant. The

Victorian building of Christ Church Sparkbrook was damaged beyond repair: trees uprooted and crashed into its roof and walls. For the congregation of Christ Church, the loss of the building, which was subsequently levelled, was a visual illustration of the changes that were inexorably creeping up on the Anglican presence in this majority Muslim parish. Dwindling congregational numbers and stretched resources were now accompanied by physical anonymity. Instead of the imposing fabric of the Victorian pile, a hastily fabricated wooden cross signalled the consecrated ground of the church plot.

We are taught as priests to accompany the dying, and death is writ large into our defining story as Christians. In an age when death is kept at arm's length and youth and vitality virtually idolized in the media, the Church clearly has a prophetic voice to speak about death done well. The destruction of the tornado was just one element in what amounted to a kind of death for the nature of Anglican presence in Sparkbrook. It would culminate in the closure of Sunday worship for Christ Church: no building and insufficient numbers conspired to bring about an ending. There was a public and communal 'dying' that seemed altogether much more problematic for us to engage with than the individual mortality we all face. The liturgies for a dying patient and grieving families at funerals were not translated into the loss and change that the congregation were feeling and encountering at the corporate level. During a funeral visit, preparing for a liturgy that helps a family 'let go', we do not dodge the 'D' word. The deceased has not 'gone away' as if popping to the corner shop for some milk. Funerals face the reality of endings, of a new life without the person who had seemed to be such a permanent fixture.

I'm reminded of T. S. Eliot's foreboding climax to his 'Journey of the Magi':

Were we led all that way for
Birth or Death? There was a Birth, certainly,
We had evidence and no doubt. I had seen birth and death,

But had thought they were different; this Birth was
Hard and bitter agony for us, like Death, our death.

'This Birth' that Eliot refers to has somehow woven into the
Christian story a narrative that charges newness with 'Hard and
bitter agony for us', and death with life. Where was the space
to talk in similar terms about the ambiguities of a decisive and
inexorable loss to Anglican parish presence?

Several years later, I took responsibility for Sparkbrook as
a Pioneer curate: that is to say, with a brief for mission and
to be part of engendering a sustainable Anglican presence in
the parish. How could we even begin to think about the business of new life without embracing something of the death that
was so evident? The schizophrenia I had been feeling as parish
priest and Pioneer curate perhaps was a 'vital' microcosm of
our priestly ministry: finding life in the very act of death.

Several years later and now priest-in-charge, the conflicted
nature of my role has not diminished. Serving in a parish where
public faith is decidedly Islamic and the Anglican presence
marginal conjures up a number of paradoxes. For many in the
community around us, a Christian witness is welcomed by all
faiths. That there are Christians serious about a life lived for God
in prayer is seen as good by Muslims, Sikhs and Hindus, and
an antidote to the moral confusion they associate with British
culture. Pioneer ministers in other contexts may feel the need
to 'dress down' and sit lightly to the public trappings of inherited parochial ministry. In Sparkbrook, however, the epitome
of post-Christian Britain (notice that this is not *secular* Britain),
the fact that there is still an Anglican priest walking the streets
in a dog collar provides a reassurance and a point of contact for
a shared Godward concern. That shared concern translates into
praying for people of other faiths in the community and being
invited to pray for families and in homes. In some ways, there
is a very old-fashioned ministry of cure of souls opening up in
new ways where a publicly available, prayerful upholding of all
people is valued for the common good.

While there is an opening up of opportunity, other avenues of ministry fade away. The broader demographic shifts have meant that the residual Christian community has contracted. There was a seven-year hiatus for the congregation without the permanence of a physical building, compounding the sense that the Anglican presence is beleaguered. The occasional offices thus constitute a fraction of my work. My colleagues in rural parishes or the suburbs may groan under the burden of funerals or have to find that delicate balance of serial baptisms in Sunday services that welcome newcomers while simultaneously fostering the sense of community of the existing congregation. For those of us ministering in parts of the inner city, such challenges can only be regarded wistfully. Some recent models of mission encourage an intentional focus on the opportunities presented by baptisms and weddings, and especially the financial possibilities of the latter. The social demographic context prohibits this from being in any way realistic.

Yet there is something purifying about this pared-down, fragile presence. There is no scope for me to instrumentalize these offices; to somehow market God through a twist and sell of baptism and marriage: offering one service while actually desiring that the customer, because that is what they then become, buy another. In the world of business, we would have shut up shop well before 2007, and declared that there was no market in Sparkbrook. Alternatively, we might have reinvented ourselves as purveyors of a niche product, high on 'quality' but really only meant for the discerning client. I thank God that the Church is *not* a business and the Diocese of Birmingham has committed to a presence in Sparkbrook that cannot be reduced to simplistic assessments of a bottom-line return.

For all that the diocesan commitment to parishes like mine speaks of a profound generosity of vocation and mission, it would be naive to assume that this can mean that the shape of priestly ministry remains unaltered. Rachel Mann has written of the pervasive imagery of models of priestly ministry forged in a bygone rural age by the likes of George Herbert and James Woodforde and how pernicious they can be to the contemporary encouragement of vocations in the urban north.[1] Those images die hard in personal and public imaginations. The pastoral idyll of a benign but largely ineffectual parish priest at the hub of community life in popular imagination can afford to be stiffened by a degree of evangelistic edge to become more appealing to prospective ordinands, but still offers little resonance to the challenges of urban ministry. BBC TV's series *Rev* has gone some way in presenting a very different vision of a church of cultural diversity, grit and numerical and financial fragility in London's inner city. But it has done this at the expense of a portrayal of the hapless Revd Adam Smallbone as a kind of King Canute, forlornly attempting to hold back an encroaching tide ready to engulf and eventually obliterate the remaining vestiges of the Church of England. The clue is in his name, and though we regard him fondly, and recognize the multitude of small joys and sorrows in his quiet dedication, the drama suggests that he does not quite have the backbone to be anything more than an anachronism.

It is at this point that I have to admit how conflicted I feel about this. The language of the market that drives withdrawal from parishes or the creep towards niche specialism is a very real possibility and temptation. My evangelicalism keeps me committed to the idea that it is good that our churches grow and that conversion and discipleship are to be sought and encouraged. This conviction remains true for me in a parish where so many of my neighbours are of another faith. The narrative of growth, sustainable numbers and finance is at least a pragmatic fact; it cannot be otherwise for the inner city, even if we were to disregard the sober warnings of diocesan secretaries. But it is not the only narrative, and I suppose that even this chapter is an effort in affirming the many different narratives of loss and change that the Church of England is needing to negotiate and be attentive to. The significance of

---

1 See Rachel Mann, 'Far from those dark satanic mills', *Church Times*, 9 January 2015.

being attentive to such narratives lies in the unique blessing that these apparently bleak prospects provide. While I have been parish priest in Sparkbrook, I have begun to learn something of a very different model of public ministry that is in the vein of the parochial vision of my inherited tradition, but has yet required its own 'death'.

The cultural and religious richness of Sparkbrook enables a shared discourse in the public language of faith and prayer. But that richness carries with it colonial memories that make the community sensitive to ulterior motives and the abuses of privileged power. My Muslim, Sikh and Hindu neighbours are attuned to any engagement from the Church of England that would seem to be exploitative or culturally supremacist. A very public Anglican presence is demanded but it is no longer under the terms of its earlier settlement.

Back in the 1980s, Roger Hooker was part of a generation of missionary priests who had returned to ministry in the UK and were anticipating the melting pot of faiths that our cities were becoming. He talked of a mission of 'loitering with intent'. He was already recognizing that the Anglican presence was not a right or a given. A patient listening and attentiveness would need to be accompanied by a readiness to share that would be impelled by invitation not presumption. This is the milieu I recognize in Sparkbrook, and see in the parishes of my neighbouring colleagues. The 'loitering' evokes something of that 'wasting time with God' that that great Dominican Herbert McCabe characterized as constitutive of prayer. It speaks of a lack of control and of the phenomenon that inevitably follows it: surprise. For if we are able to dictate the nature of the engagement with a community on our terms, surprise is going to be a rare commodity.

Is not this what we are doing when we as priests sit with people through and in the midst of that ultimate sign of our human condition, death, but trusting to God who is ultimately in control? This is by no means saying that the parish presence should be consigned to passive resignation to decline. Rather, it is a recognition that the *form* of that presence has so changed that our prayerful 'intent' as we loiter cannot be pre-planned and packaged. Parochial church councils requiring treasurers and minute-takers, musicians for Sunday worship, volunteers for Sunday school and professionals to support the running of community trusts or lead fundraising are among the machinery of Anglican presence under serious threat. I know of inner-city parishes with congregations that exceed fifty in number but where the wage-earners are fewer than ten, including the priest. There are financial burdens that make the ongoing sustainability of a number of parish churches untenable, confirming that the pattern of a priest for each parish is a dead-letter in urban as well as rural areas. Sparkbrook is not alone in experiencing a fundamental shift in the conception of parochial ministry that is outside of the control of the Church.

I believe that it is some of the defining features of the inherited tradition that will help us negotiate this new vista of fragile establishment. There remains within that motif of 'loitering' something of the need for physical presence; to still be in the neighbourhood. Despite the learning that the Church needs to take on board about networked relationships, there seems to be something intrinsic to the Christian community and ecclesial identity that is rooted in place. As Andrew Davison and Alison Milbank highlight in *For the Parish*,[2] the embodiment of the good news in the gathered church serving and blessing a particular place is axiomatic to our story. But that is not the whole story, and it is in the embodied reality of inner-city fragility that new ways of being present are being re-imagined.

Two years ago I conducted the funeral of a baby that was stillborn. The mum, who I will call Serena, was devastated and the funeral director advised me that she wanted the church to lead a funeral for her baby but was nervous about what a vicar might do: that her grief might not be treated seriously. Serena was a young Afro-Caribbean woman whose parents

---

2 Andrew Davison and Alison Milbank, *For the Parish: A Critique of Fresh Expressions* (London: SCM Press, 2013).

had attended church, while she herself had just a vague sense that she needed to commit her child to God's care. Serena's boyfriend was distancing himself from all this, wanting to get things over with quickly and with as little emotional fuss as possible. We talked about how to mark the preciousness of this tiny life, and to acknowledge the rupture of its loss. Serena wanted to bring some balloons, and after the committal let them go as a symbol of releasing the baby to God.

As I waited at the cemetery among the plots designated for stillbirths, a taxi trundled to a stop by the manicured lawns. Serena tottered to the graveside in her high heels, holding fast to the strings of three coloured helium balloons while her boyfriend stood back, impassive behind his sunglasses. I read the prayers, grateful for their ballast at this most lonely of funerals. I was wondering what Serena would make of the Scriptures, feeling vulnerable facing the magnitude of her grief but without the buffer of a congregation to swell the sense of occasion. As I read the prayers, I think it was the first time in my life that I truly understood what it meant to inhabit the liturgy. The gravity of Scripture was a felt weight lending articulacy to a pain and hope that can all too easily be rendered inarticulate by a surfeit of our own words. In the spaces between the prayers, we held silence, *being* before our Creator. After the committal, I drew her boyfriend closer to the grave and suggested he just hold Serena while we prepared for the release of the balloons. There was an absurd moment when we realized that trees were obscuring the air above the grave so we walked to a higher point and I said another brief prayer. Serena let go of the strings, blew a kiss and we all laughed through tears as the balloons rose and then careered to one side with a gust of wind and lodged under the branch of a tree.

Five minutes must have elapsed as Serena waited patiently, watching, as each balloon was gradually dislodged in the breeze and lifted, shrinking into the clouds. She turned to me, eyes full of tears but smiling: 'Father, it always takes longer than you think; but they go in the end.'

I have frequently pondered over that funeral and what was happening that day: the various negotiations that were taking place as Serena found a safe space to embody her loss and to affirm her child's significance in the language of God's love in Christ. In the following weeks, I bumped into her several times and she invited me to pray for her to conceive again, and then to bless her new sporty hatchback, bought as a gift to herself from a series of extra shifts at the care home where she worked. Several months later, I found out that Serena had moved away, following a familiar pattern of migration away from Sparkbrook, leaving no forwarding address. As I reflect on our encounters, I can't but see a microcosm of the challenges and joys of parochial ministry today. It was as if all my reserves were stripped down to the barest offer of hope at the point of death. I could not escape the vivid imagery of scarcity: the tiny grave, our small huddle of mourners, the bald words of the liturgy. Yet we had encountered God; all of us.

I offered to drive Serena and her boyfriend back home after the funeral and as they got out of the car she asked me to get out too, then clasped me in a huge hug of gratitude. I too had been surprised by God's comfort at a point of genuine inadequacy. I wonder about those balloons, and my dread as I saw them skip under the boughs of the tree, trapped, while Serena was unperturbed, just waiting: 'but they go in the end'. I have to admit to a terrible desire to be in control; to want to make things happen just as they are planned. It is never entirely clear to me at what point my very worthy desire to see Sparkbrook being transformed and the church community grow, to baptize new Christians and be part of a story of regeneration and renewal, drifts into a desire for control. I suspect I just need to wait, like Serena, and watch, having done all I can, but no more.

Admitting that ministry is inevitably changing, and that parish priests will need to encourage change, there are yet those moments, as I experienced at the graveside with Serena, that bring a sharp focus to what we are about that we dare not relinquish: an open-handed availability to anyone in need, and that contemplative, prayerful being before God. I wonder whether we are often offered a false choice between tradition and change. One of the 'gifts' the inner-city parish has to offer the wider Church is an example of change because there is no other option. The option, rather, that we do have seems to be whether that change, effectively dying to certain conceptions of the Anglican parish, is pursued in ways that remain under-girded by contemplative prayer and the free concern for any in need in the place where we are called to minister.

I think of the elderly Afro-Caribbean Christians in Birmingham's inner city and the stories they have told me about arriving in Britain in the 1950s. Sparkbrook looked like a huge factory, apparently, because what else were all those chimneys for? There are stories of cold weather and colder welcomes, where even the memories seem to be soaked in black and white tones, devoid of colour. If they have not already moved away, they are part of neighbourhoods that have changed beyond recognition. Their stories are replete with experiences of dislocation offering a tantalizing prophetic voice to the Church of England that cannot afford to lose its rootedness and yet must learn the grief of loss. Some of the remaining elderly Christian minority have embraced experiences such as having their shopping done by Muslim neighbours more attuned to communal responsibility than so-called Christian areas in the suburbs. Recalling again McCabe's 'wasting time with God', I take him to be describing the necessary pointlessness of silence, and the indispensable uselessness of the reading of Scripture. The 'giftedness' of the Church, in its true meaning as a people enlivened by God and freely offered to the world, dictates that contemplative practices are more than items in the 'to-do list' of clergy: they speak of our essence. As Rowan Williams has written, 'the Church is, absurdly, both necessary and unnecessary'.[3] Prayer is the paradigmatic act of relinquishment where

---

3 Rowan Williams, 'Afterword', in Frances Ward and Sarah Coakley (eds), *Fear & Friendship: Anglicans Engaging with Islam* (London: Continuum, 2012), p. 149.

we commit to the control of God and refuse the anxieties that come with asserting our own usefulness. It seems to me that many Anglican parishes are having to relinquish much, and the pressure to operate out of anxiety is profound. I look inside myself at my response to the completion of mission strategies and parish returns that monitor attendance and financial giving and feel the burden of institutional expectation; but must again release this in prayer. This sometimes feels like a daily decision to die to the expectations that I put on myself as much as they are placed on me by the institution. In this light, the binary opposition of a catholic contemplative spirituality and an evangelical intention in mission seems wholly inadequate.

In July 2014 Sparkbrook was rocked by a gang murder just a hundred metres from the new church building, built after an interval of seven years. A number of us had been meeting in the church on that early summer evening and witnessed the perpetrators walk away from the scene, bloodied. Later that evening, I received an email from a local community leader asking if the church could be used for a delegation of community representatives to meet with police and to then issue a statement to the press the next day. The Church of England had been invited to be the focus for the wider community's grief and trauma, hosting a gathering of different faith leaders, politicians and NGO leaders, as well as the police. The invitation was unexpected, unasked for, and represented a trust in the Church's ability to be a safe space for all. Something inimitably parochial was happening in Sparkbrook that was the fruit of investment in relationships, in patient and public care for the common good.

I remain unsure about the future for ministry in Sparkbrook. There are few signs that the parish will be able to sustain buildings and clergy without anything less than an investment from outside the parish by the Diocese. All I know is that in parishes like mine we are discovering death and resurrection, relinquishment and renewal, in deeply moving ways. Such narratives have a part in the wider purposes of the Church of England and are a gift and reproach to a strictly utilitarian vision of mission. My hope is that across our dioceses there will still be space for the profligate and the extravagant. Such intentions chime with my instinct to marry the contemplative with the missional even if they may perpetuate institutional uncertainty. I keep holding to that image of 'loitering', occasionally consciously prayer-walking the parish as a sign and symbol of that motif. The complaints from clergy who feel squeezed by a multitude of demands, those for whom prayer itself ends up becoming a luxury, are well-worn but genuinely held. What we cannot afford, though, is to sacrifice the practices of prayer and contemplation to an idol of institutional self-preservation. If waiting in prayer means that other things are left undone, then so be it.

As I write this, sitting in the church office, I can hear the laughter and chatter of our weekly women's group. This is a mix of Christian and Muslim women who meet to do some physical exercise, eat together and share crafts in our café area. This particular ministry is a world away from the comfortable clichés of garden fetes. Prayer and the language of faith are integral to the friendships and conversations, and there is a robust acknowledgement of the universal claims made by the respective traditions. Though we long for others to become Christians (and the transparency of such hope is another gift of our context because there is an equal desire to see the conversion of Christians to Islam), we dare not put a price on our investment in the common good. Even so, we are beginning to see journeys of discipleship: stumbling steps towards the recognition of Christ who relinquished all that we may know, too, the transfiguration of death into new life. In my better moments, the embrace of absence experienced in inner-city parochial ministry becomes the ground for God's abundant presence.

Office: Baptism

MATTHEW BULLIMORE

Royston, South Yorkshire

Speaking from a context where baptism is in huge demand but virtually unlinked from continuing discipleship, Matthew Bullimore ponders the sacramental and biblical theology of baptism as seeds of grace sown in a community landscape, awaiting an unexpected flourishing.

The young woman was waiting to cross the road. I recognized her because she had been baptized a couple of weeks before, along with her three-year-old son. I had wondered if it was something to do with the church primary school (which does not in fact make baptism an entrance requirement). I wasn't going to tell her that. Nor was I going to turn her away for coming for merely pragmatic reasons – I do not think there are many outright poor reasons for wanting to have your child baptized (more on that later). I had seen on the baptism application form that she was not baptized and asked her if she would like to be. If she wanted her little boy to be brought up in the faith then perhaps she would think about becoming a member of the church too. As often happens, she said she did not want to distract from the little one's big day. I persuaded her and I think they came to one of the monthly baptism preparation evenings.

The young woman stopped me and told me in very broad Yorkshire how much she enjoyed the service. My vicar-ego inevitably began to swell. I was very pleased, I told her. It was so good to have them with us. She replied, 'Yeah, it were right nice. So nice I even thought about convertin'.' The green man appeared and off she went chuckling at such a funny idea, my vicar-ego a tattered and smouldering ruin blowing down the street as I whispered to her departing frame, 'You ... just ... have.'

I would dearly love to be baptizing people who have come to faith and who are regular – even frequent – worshippers. Yet people in my parishes coming for baptism, like this young woman, do not usually come to promise a commitment to Christ. They don't expect to introduce the child into the regular worshipping life of the church. The vital ingredients of faith, understanding and commitment, seem to be missing. I accept that somewhere along the line I had failed to help her to see what baptism was all about. For her it was not about a conversion of life and a turning of the heart and mind. Having an open policy had failed. The strongly voluntarist supposition, with which I am in some sympathy, is that we should expect a decision to turn to Christ to be made with integrity and faithfulness. We should expect the promises made by parents and godparents to be kept so that the child is brought up in the faith. These are fair and reasonable expectations – but nevertheless I want to argue forcefully for the blessings that an open baptism policy brings.

I am aware of much best practice when it comes to preparation and follow-up – in the work of Ally Barrett and of Mark Earey, for example. Yet we are not at a stage in our common life as a parish where we have the resources to offer it. We have about 125 baptisms a year. We baptize on Sunday, the day of new creation and resurrection, outside the seasons of Lent and Advent, which amounts to about three baptisms a week. We cannot baptize that number of people in the main service (as we are canonically obliged to do) because it would swamp our congregations. Often each baptism party will want to bring between fifty and a hundred guests. Some at least will talk (and text) throughout the service. So we offer them bespoke services in the afternoon.

This is what one looks like. At 1.58 p.m. the families and friends walk through the door. The women are dressed apparently to go clubbing. The men are in their best shirts and shoes. Hair has been styled. The child is in a fancy white suit or dress. An effort has been made; there is a sense of occasion. As people often remark, the christening is the new wedding. It is a celebration among friends of family life. As they enter I gauge how much of a struggle the service is going to be. This judgement includes a consideration of the volume of the guests' conversation and whether they have all come in together from the hostelry over the road. I make the judgement so that I know how to pitch the service.

It begins. Mum is on the phone trying to get the godparents out of the pub. The lads are texting on the back row. I swallow my pride and do a back-and-forth comic number on the responses, to make sure that they know what to do. I tell them in my sermon about John the Baptist – the patron of one of the parishes and its church school. I focus on the symbols used in the baptism service and how they tie into the story. I make the most of the liturgy's symbolic action. Eventually, wrung out and hoarse, exhilarated and joyful, I wave people goodbye as they clutch their certificates and godparent cards. I do not expect to see them in church again until the next family baptism, funeral or wedding.

Is this a 'baptizing' of what has become essentially secular ritual? It seems worth observing that the woman waiting at the crossing *had* realized that the service was about 'conversion' (whatever she understood by that). Something had challenged her. We had made a connection. A door was open.

I certainly see in her response a challenge for us to do more in terms of preparation and follow-up. But I also see good in people's continuing desire for baptism. Even if they do not yet 'convert', there is something that makes them at least pause and think as they hear *and see* the gospel. The contention of this chapter is that those natural desires that bring them to us for baptism can gracefully be focused and refined – perfected

– by the performance of this sacrament. In an increasingly unchurched environment, baptism is a means of grace and preparatory for the further work of sanctification. It is a beginning.

In what follows I examine the accounts of the baptism of Jesus in the Gospels in order to see what they reveal about what is happening in the Church's baptism. I interrogate the dynamics of grace and faith to see who is acting, what is revealed and what this might mean for our own culture. I argue that Christian baptism is strong and pliant enough to include more than just the important focus on the faith of the new and committed worshipper (the voluntarist model). It presents us with an opportunity to see the way that grace is working – slowly, gradually and effectively – within a local community.[1]

The baptism of Jesus

The story of Jesus' baptism may be foundational but it is also unique rather than exemplary. Two separate baptisms are invoked, the baptism of John preparing for the baptism that he promises will be brought by the stronger one coming after him: 'I have baptized you with water; but he will baptize you with the Holy Spirit' (Mark 1.8; Acts 19.1–7). Yet the baptism of John is not the baptism of the Church, nor is Jesus baptized as the first Christian. How could the sinless one undergo a baptism of repentance in preparation for the forgiveness of sins? Yet he asks to be baptized.

Instead, the narratives are **revelatory**. The Father declares that this is the beloved Son with whom he is well pleased, and we are made witnesses of a divine relationship. It is one, as we shall see, into which we are drawn by filiation through our baptism. The narratives reveal that the knowledge we have of the triune God is first and foremost a personal knowing. It is

---

1 I am immensely grateful to Jessica Martin and Ally Barrett for excellent and helpful advice while writing this chapter.

about trust and faith in the Son sent by the Father as his Spirit comes to rest on us. Knowledge of God is by no means just a set of beliefs to which we must assent. Instead, the baptism of Jesus reveals to us the mystery of God's life and the nature of God as love. The revelation is of a relationship into which we are called.

The Gospel narratives of Jesus' baptism come with a hinterland of meaning derived from the Messianic expectations of Second Temple Judaism. Mark uses quotations from Malachi and Isaiah to preface the account of the baptism to show that John comes to prepare the way for Jesus (Mark 1.2–3; Mal. 3.1; Isa. 40.3). John is uncommonly successful; the 'whole Judean countryside and all the people of Jerusalem' come to be baptized and confess their sins. The entire nation turns up. Mark's hyperbole works to suggest that all need to partake of John's prophetic sign and so prepare for the coming one. We do not know why they come but they discern a need for something new to happen. They respond to John's preaching and realize they have a desire for forgiveness. So John's baptism is **preparatory**. There is a desire that is *not yet* faith drawing people to John. John brings them to a point of confession and readiness as they show desire to see the one who is coming.

But a question presents itself here. Does the whole nation receiving John's baptism also receive the baptism that will come by way of the stronger one, the baptism with the Holy Spirit? Is John speaking still to all when he says 'He will baptize you with the Holy Spirit'? Who will actually receive the Holy Spirit and a second baptism? How far is the Spirit's reach? Mark remains very quiet about that – and then, intriguingly, we realize that Jesus baptizes no one. In John's Gospel the Baptist's followers think that Jesus is baptizing, but we learn that it is his followers who are doing it (John 3.26; 4.2).

There is also a significant difference over the nature of that further baptism. Mark's phrase is expanded (in the Q tradition) in Matthew (3.11), and in Luke (3.16) where it is promised that the stronger one will baptize them with 'the Holy Spirit *and fire*. Christians both early and late have seen this in terms of Pentecost, where the Spirit manifests like tongues of fire (Acts 1.5). Others down the ages have been more attuned to the apparent threat of Messianic judgement, encouraged by John's subsequent claim that the stronger one will, with winnowing fork in hand, gather the wheat but burn the chaff with unquenchable fire (Matt. 3.12). For John, it seems, the Messiah's baptism promises either blessing or judgement, either Spirit or fire. Either way, the baptism he brings will be purgative – it will be for the reform of those who accept it or for the destruction of those who do not.

John should be aligned, however, with the great prophetic tradition that holds together the purgative and the restorative without necessarily seeing them as opposed. Often water, fire, breath and Spirit in both their purgative and restorative aspects are brought together (e.g. Num. 31.23; Isa. 44.3–4; 4.3–4; Ezek. 36.25–27; Mal. 3.2–4). Future blessing, renewal, refreshment by water in the wilderness, re-creation, spiritual outpouring and even fiery purging can be held together as goods that the nation will undergo or receive.

Given that in the Q tradition John clearly expects that the one who follows will bring not just spiritual blessing but alongside it fiery judgement, it is no wonder that the imprisoned John sends word to ask if Jesus is the Messiah. Perhaps there had been rather less of the eschatological judgement and fiery purging in Jesus' ministry than he had foreseen. John, in apocalyptic mood, is still waiting for the imminent end of the present age. Jesus' response is to proclaim that the new age has begun; it is breaking in now:

> Go and tell John what you hear and see: the blind receive their sight, the lame walk, the lepers are cleansed, the deaf hear, the dead are raised, and the poor have good news brought to them. And blessed is anyone who takes no offence at me. (Matt. 11.4–6)

Where, then, does this leave judgement and the baptism of fire? The Gospel accounts do not set aside this frightening aspect of baptism. In fact, Jesus was alluding in the passage above to a prophecy of Isaiah that links renewal in the wilderness with judgement. God is coming with vengeance and terrible recompense even as he is coming to save (Isa. 35.1–7). Yet, where is this fiery judgement to be seen in the Gospel? Or more precisely, who is judged and who undergoes the effects of that judgement?

It is Jesus who is both the baptizer and the one baptized. 'I came to bring fire to the earth, and how I wish it were already kindled! I have a baptism with which to be baptized, and what stress I am under until it is completed' (Luke 12.49–50). Jesus' life and death pronounces a **judgement** on the present age, its sinfulness, its cultures of death and isolation; but it is the effects of that judgement that *he himself will undergo for us* as the new age breaks in. The second baptism is **vicarious**: the theological stress here is on the work of Christ and not yet on us.

Even in Mark, where we do not expect a second baptism of fire, it is clear that Jesus sees his suffering and death as a baptism to which he will submit. It is nonetheless, as he tells James and John, a baptism in which they will share (Mark 10.38–40): 'The cup that I drink you will drink; and with the baptism with which I am baptized, you will be baptized.'

It is not a long leap from here to Paul where baptism is described in fully incorporative terms:

Do you not know that all of us who have been baptized into Christ Jesus were baptized into his death? Therefore we have been buried with him by baptism into death, so that, just as Christ was raised from the dead by the glory of the Father, so we too might walk in newness of life. (Rom. 6.3–4)

Baptism becomes for us a way of participating in the life, death and resurrection of Christ (cf. Gal. 3.27). If, for Paul, baptism is seen as an initiation into Christ then it is because Jesus seems to have understood his own life and Passion as a baptism into suffering and death on behalf of others but also as one in which we come to participate, living a Christoform life.

This baptism is not just vicarious but **incorporative**. The grace, life and blessing that are effectually conferred in this baptism are received because Christ is the faithful actor who accomplishes salvation in his life, Passion and resurrection. Yet we are made Christ-like – we participate in his life – through God's action in us.

Who receives this second spiritual baptism; this baptism that incorporates us into the Christ who has accomplished our salvation? How far does it reach? Morna Hooker argues that Jesus' whole ministry in Mark's Gospel is to be seen as the means by which the people are baptized with the Spirit (cf. Rom. 8.11). After his baptism Jesus cannot be regarded as being without the Spirit that rests on him. By the work of Jesus upon whom the Spirit rests the people are plunged into the sphere of God's purifying, restorative and creative power.

Faith in Jesus' ability to forgive, heal and save is crucial for experiencing that power but it is a frail and unfocused faith for all that (e.g. Mark 9.22–24). Note that in Mark few people are able to acknowledge who Jesus really is – while the judgement falls upon the unclean spirits who do recognize him (Mark 3.20–30). Of those who truly recognize him, Peter is the first as they travel to Caesarea Philippi (Mark 8.29), but even he fails to understand Jesus' foretelling of his Passion. By the end of the Gospel it is the Gentile centurion at the cross who is the first to bear witness to Jesus' divine Sonship. No one else makes the profession that is heard when Jesus is baptized – that he is the beloved Son of God. Yet those who encounter Jesus experience the holy work of purgation: the possessed are relieved of all that oppresses them and the demoniacs are restored to health and to society. Here we see the second baptism as something **re-creational**, liberative and restorative: it is something that brings about new creation in the Spirit despite the frailness of our faith. The inbreaking of the age to come into the here and now means that human lives, societies and cultures can be transformed through the rule of Christ. Moreover, this baptism **elicits faith**. In Mark, although some small measure of trusting faith marks an entry into relationship with Jesus, he does not demand a full understanding of who he is in order for people to receive his blessings. Those who are drawn to him are not turned away and the encounter with Jesus elicits trust and the confession of who Jesus is.

Baptism in church

How does the baptism of the Church resonate with the foundational narratives in the Gospels? Do these reflections help us with the questions raised by an open baptism policy?

The decision: baptism as preparatory

The narratives of Jesus' baptism put solely elective and voluntarist understandings of baptism under some pressure. The people who come to John do not come with a fixed idea of what they desire. Yet faith – in some form – is working in those people. Some inner promptings, some as yet unarticulated and unformed desires, bring them out of their usual daily lives to the banks of the Jordan.

I see it as a sign of grace that people are still drawn to seek the Church's baptism. After all, it is not quite something that we could advertise like a coffee morning. When I ask, people give any number of reasons why they have come. The reasons given, while not explicitly confessional and not the answers that catechisms might expect, have an integrity and tend to point to the fundamental welfare of the child. Many tell me that they come from a family in which baptism has always played a part, and although they find it hard to say why, they want to affirm that tradition and give their own child an opportunity to enjoy its benefits. For some it means a kind of divine protection.

Some may come for the same reason that they will bring the children to Messy Church or hope for a place at the church school, deeming exposure to a Christian ethos to be beneficial. While that does not necessarily mean that they expect to come to church, they seek a culture and an education for the child that points beyond the cultures of which they are a part. For some the reasons are those of feeling. To whom can thanks be offered when a gift so precious has been given – after a difficult pregnancy or birth, for example? These are by no means trivial, poor or 'wrong' reasons.

They are, however, not necessarily the 'right' reasons either. The Church is called to help reorient the world to its true end. The celebration of a baptism rearticulates some of those desires. Baptism is about family tradition – but this is a family where water is thicker than blood. Baptism is about receiving a name, for here we are called, as this particular person, at this particular time, to be a part of God's story. In baptism we do not receive invulnerability, but we do begin to share in a life that has already defeated death. Baptism inducts us into a way of life that is distinctively Christian and it may set us free from some of the demands and constraints of the dominant culture. The desires we have for our children are now set within the context of faith in the living God.

This reorienting of desire we might call repentance. It is about a turning. It is easy enough to link this to parents and godparents making decisions about the way of life they have chosen for the child. John tells people that they can turn away from what they want to leave behind and towards Jesus approaching to meet them. The decision re-enacts this turning – away from all that separates us from God and one another, and towards Christ.

The signing with the cross: baptism as redemptive judgement

The signing with the cross follows from the decision. The child is claimed by Christ as one of his own and receives the sign – an invisible tattoo – of God's loving self-offering for us. The emphasis is on the cross, on what Christ has done *for* us and that we could not do for ourselves. It is what makes possible our turning from the darkness of sin to the light of new life. Together, the decision and the signing with the cross presume a judgement; a judgement upon a world that refuses grace, and a judgement for a world of which Christ is king.

The giving of the lighted candle: baptism as re-creational

It is the Church's work to create a culture in which people are given the opportunity to be attracted to Christ in the first place. Such a culture is produced by the visible quality of a church's common life, by the services it provides in the community, by the pastoral care it gives and by its proclamation of the gospel in evangelism and mission. It may prompt some to come for baptism as if coming to the altar of a god not quite unknown. I would argue that being hospitable is one means of creating that culture.

Rather than making an easy distinction between those who are in and those who are out, the Church has a ministry of hospitality to those who are under the priest's cure of souls. By welcoming those who come for baptism, the Church is witnessing to the God who is already at work in people's lives and who always wants to offer us so much more. It is a work that bears witness to Christ's re-creation of the world.

The lighted candle is a sign that speaks of witness and cultural transformation. Light shines in the darkness, and it is the light of life. As baptized Christians we are called to take the light of Christ into a world that we all recognize can be very dark indeed. Giving the candle is an opportunity to talk about the resurrection. On Good Friday the church is dark and bare because Jesus has died. On the day of resurrection, the first disciples go to the tomb at dawn and find that he is not there; he has been raised. Light has returned to the world, so on Easter morning we bring the Paschal candle into the dark church. How will the godparents help the candidate to share the light? We should expect that what has been seen and heard – and indeed what has happened – in the church on the baptismal day will be good news for the life of the wider community. The child is, after all, bursting with new life, shining with light and bearing the Spirit.

The baptism in water: baptism as incorporative

John honours those who come; he takes whatever reasons they have for coming and proclaims that their hopes will be fulfilled in Jesus. It is a surprise for John when he sees how those hopes are fulfilled, and we ought to be ready to be surprised too at how God works in our parishes.

The practice of infant baptism once presumed baptism into a Christian culture that already existed within the family and in wider society – and it was within that culture that the child would grow and receive the faith. Infant baptism in particular relied on an understanding of faith as culturally mediated, formational for Christian life. Infants were not baptized only to become *true* believers later. They were baptized into a community and a way of life that was to form them from the beginning into the likeness of Christ. Faith was not private but shared between a community with its own sets of practices, its foundational stories and its common beliefs.

Many of these supports are now gone. The Christian culture and its faith community may not even include the godparents, strange as it is to say. However, in the case of infant baptism in particular, we participate in a sacrament that is supremely about the grace given to someone who cannot yet profess the faith for themselves. It is Christ's baptism that the child will share. It is his action, his faithfulness, his triumph into which the Spirit incorporates that child. It may be that the church – which may no longer have easy access to the child's everyday community – has to hold the faith on behalf of those who are baptized and hope that through repeated encounter (for example at school) they may continually be exposed to that faith in action.

The washing in water is the high point of the service and it allows us to teach about our incorporation into the life, death and resurrection of Jesus. In the Scriptures, the passage through water is a passage through danger and (the threat of) death into new life (Noah, Jonah, Moses). We pass through this water, washing off our old self, washing off even death as we pass through the grave, and we rise to new life with Jesus. We affirm eternal life already won for us and beginning now.

The chrismation: baptism as participatory in the triune relationship

If baptism is about grace then it is about God at work in us. John testified that the greater one would baptize people with the Holy Spirit. The anointing of the child with the oil of chrism witnesses to the child's reception of the Spirit. At this point we can affirm how the Spirit will make us more like Jesus if we let her. We will learn to love others as Jesus did and see the world as he did. As those chosen by God to serve others, we are anointed – christed – just as are priests, the confirmed and the monarch.

In his baptism, Jesus identifies with us so that we might be blessed by sharing in the Spirit who rests upon his body. The Church understands that he hallows the waters of baptism, incorporating us into the community of love that is the Trinity. As Eugene Rogers argues, in his baptism by John, Jesus receives as human what he has eternally as God. What he receives is the gift of the Spirit who rests on him, and by God's grace we see it. We are granted a vision of the intra-Trinitarian relations into which we are called to participate. As the Spirit 'dilates' the Trinity to make 'space' for us, and as the Spirit rests on us now as members of Christ, then we are elected to be witnesses too. In other words, baptism does not draw us out of the world but the world into the life of God.

Concluding remarks

I argue three things. First, that the role of the church is to perform the prophetic work of the Baptist. It welcomes the presence of those who come to it, for whatever reason, and points them to Jesus. The service itself should begin to make sense of the inchoate desires that bring people to this place. Second, the church administers the sacrament of baptism as an effective sign of God's love. It has, by grace, the potential to interpret our lives in the light of his gospel and to reveal our true end in him. Third, in its hospitality, and alongside the church's other work in that place, it spreads a participatory relationship of faith. In too narrow an elective, voluntary model of baptism, we run the risk of demanding too much of those who come to us and frustrating the initial grace that has brought them to the church door.

The baptism with the Spirit is not something that either the person baptized or the church can control or command. The Spirit's reach is greater than ours. The work of judgement, redemption and new creation has already been accomplished by Jesus and in the power of the Spirit we witness to it. That is our calling. By means of this efficacious sacramental sign we believe that all can be given a share in the life of the triune God. We are granted by grace that which humanity cannot have simply by nature. It is our hope that no one will be unaffected and that little by little by little the whole world is being seduced by the love of God. Whether or not the people we baptize join the worshipping community either now or later is, of course, impossible to judge. They have already come to the church and they may come again. If the parish church is effective then they will continue to be exposed to the lives of those in the Christian community with whom they dwell.

Perhaps you would like to know what happened to the woman I met at the lights? I would love to tell you that she comes to church, but she moved out of the village. Her son comes to the church school where he encounters a 'Christian ethos' by coming to regular worship, experiencing Christian teaching and, I hope, seeing Christian practices modelled. The next time I see her picking him up I will make the effort to see how she is and try to bring the conversation round to her baptism.

Is an open baptism policy useless? It is as useless as blessing and as invisible as love. I believe that it continues to leaven our culture with the ministry of the Church and exposes people, however fleetingly, to their true end in that most gratuitous of all activities, the enjoyment of God.

The Priest Attends to the Eucharist: A Tale of Two Cities

EDMUND NEWEY

Oxford and Handsworth, Birmingham

Edmund Newey meditates upon the Eucharist as a deep and transformative gift of place-centred hospitality in two very different communities: one plural and diverse, part of the lively, undefended sprawl of a Midlands city; the other more apparently circumscribed and protected, yet internationally visible.

In the summer of 2013 I moved with my family from north-west Birmingham to central Oxford; from the cultural diversity of Handsworth to the architectural splendour of Christ Church; from a place whose name evokes memories of riots and unrest to a dual foundation of College and Cathedral that exudes a timeless air of effortless superiority. 'What a contrast,' people say, and most of the time I find myself agreeing.

Yet the difference shouldn't be overdrawn. By train the two cities are only a couple of hours apart; by most geographical measures, climate, altitude, soil and bedrock, these two south Midlands settlements are hard to differentiate; and culturally they are much closer than people imagine: Oxford is now hardly less diverse than other contemporary British cities and the *hijab* is not unknown even on Christ Church's Tom Quad.

The chief undeniable difference between Birmingham and Oxford is in the ways they perceive themselves. This is seen most sharply in the contrast between the parts of the two cities that I know best: Handsworth and Christ Church. One sees itself as down to earth, ordinary and, for all the justified local pride, undervalued; the other sees itself as set apart and, with a redeeming tinge of liberal angst, special. Christ Church has almost half a million paying visitors each year; Birmingham, let alone Handsworth, scarcely registers on the Visit England website.

In this chapter I explore these continuities and differences theologically. More specifically I look at the two communities in which I have lived, worked and prayed, through the lens of the Eucharist. The sacrament is more than a way of worshipping God; it is a way of seeing ourselves anew. Throughout Christian history the Eucharist has been understood as a means of reconceiving ourselves and our context in relationship with God: reforming our perceptions of *who* we are, renewing our readiness to embrace *where* we are, letting ourselves be reshaped as individuals and as community. As William Cavanaugh has written, 'The Eucharist is the true "politics", as Augustine saw, because it is the public performance of the true eschatological City of God in the midst of another City which is passing away.'[1]

In what follows I seek to explore how this eucharistic politics helps us to discern what matters most in the common life of the *polis* in the cities of Birmingham and Oxford. In the background lies a little book by the Anglican priest Geoffrey Howard: *Dare to Break Bread: The Eucharist in Desert and City*. Written over twenty years ago, this book is a classic of Anglican parochial spirituality that stands alongside the work of Alan Ecclestone and W. H. Vanstone. It juxtaposes the author's experience of a retreat in a hermitage on Mount Assékrem in the Hoggar mountains of Algeria with his ministry in inner-city Salford. Acknowledging that his own liturgical default setting leaves 'the Eucharist locked in Church', Howard travels to Charles de Foucauld's desert hermitage to contemplate 'the challenges

1 William Cavanaugh, *Torture and Eucharist* (Oxford: Blackwell, 1998), p. 14.

which the Eucharist presents to the Christian community'. There he discovers Christ, revealed and hidden, in different ways but in equal measure, as much in the deserts of Salford as those of the Sahara:

> Though [Charles de Foucauld] had infrequent contact with other Christians, his passion for the Eucharist, the most communal of all acts of worship, was stronger than any I have heard or read about. Yet paradoxically, he chose to live where he would rarely share bread and wine with others. It is to this same desert place that I have come to contemplate the challenges which the Eucharist presents to the Christian community. I am putting on Eucharistic spectacles and viewing disparate events of my past from this extraordinary vantage point.
>
> ...
>
> I hold the bread in my hand and see there the God who created, sustains and saves the world. I see food for the hungry, strength for the weak, power for the powerless. I am not bothered whether bread has become body or whether it remains plain bread. Let the theologians argue. Those issues are as sterile as the stones of this place. All I know is that I look at bread but see God.[2]

Handsworth is not Salford, Christ Church is certainly not Assékrem, and I would characterize neither of the places with which this chapter is concerned as a desert. Yet celebrating the Eucharist, as president and as a member of the congregation, in these two places, has helped me to appreciate both the distinct specificity of the two contexts and their people and the continuity between them. To anticipate my conclusion, the daily repetition of the Eucharist celebration is revelatory: it yields a fuller appreciation of the uniqueness of a particular place and

---

2 Geoffrey Howard, *Dare to Break Bread: The Eucharist in Desert and City* (London: DLT, 1992), pp. ix, 48.

its charisms and of the uniqueness of the universal Christ who unites all places in himself

I'll begin with Geoffrey Howard's question, one that struck me sharply on moving to Oxford: is the Eucharist locked in the cathedral here? On the face of it this is the unpalatable truth about the liturgy in Oxford's mother church. Here where we celebrate the Eucharist, in a holy sanctuary behind the double threshold of an imposing college gate and the cathedral's west doors, are we not especially susceptible to Geoffrey Howard's criticism? By exploring the anthropological functions of Tom Quad and the theological resonances of the Eucharist as celebrated here, I hope to indicate that this may not be the case. I will then compare this with my experience of the daily Eucharist in Handsworth: how it interacts with the concerns of the community and helps reshape the ways in which we see and respond. Finally I consider the Eucharist as a school of attentiveness to God, the world and one another. In each time and place we can learn anew that, engaging in this apparently most inward-facing of ecclesial activities, we may in fact be at our most open and outward-looking.

Tom Quad

Unlike the rocks of Mount Assékrem and the concrete of Salford, the stones of Tom Quad feel far from sterile. Christ Church's front quadrangle is perhaps the prime piece of central Oxford real estate, the background to countless tourist photographs and student pranks, layered with cultural and historical mean-ing. The simplest way to articulate what it is like to live and work on Tom Quad is to describe it as a privilege. It certainly is that, but it is also much more: a schooling in the subtleties of human interaction with a built environment. Sitting at my desk I hear on a daily basis the range of reactions evoked by this architecture: the booming voices of hearty sportsmen and women, the anxious whispers of interview candidates on the

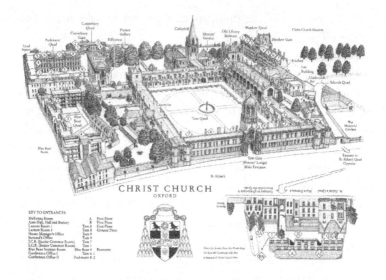

CHRIST CHURCH
OXFORD

mobile to their parents, the exaggerated embraces of alumni returning to greet their contemporaries. Tom Quad lays bare hidden aspects of our personalities: how people carry themselves in it – slinking close to the walls, strutting, strolling, sprinting and sprawling; how they respond to it – with everything from touching admiration to chippy resentment, arrogant entitlement and cringing unworthiness.

The origins of Oxford's quadrangles and Cambridge's courts lie in the monastic cloister, a place of study, meditation and exercise. As they have evolved in the collegiate universities, quadrangles have retained more than a vestige of those purposes, but to them has been added a key social role. Quadrangles are not parade grounds or gardens or car parks, yet they are perhaps the central community-forming space in a college's topography, and encounters on their pathways are central to the smooth functioning of the institution. In utilitarian terms college quadrangles appear to be a terrible waste of space and resources, but physically, practically and imaginatively they are at the heart of a college's life and identity.

This, of course, is the insider's perspective. The outsider tends to have a rather different response. The outsider's vision of Tom Quad is of an enticing green oasis glimpsed through an opening from a crowded street. These glimpses are part of the magic of Oxford and Cambridge, but they also stoke the inevitable sense of stratification: these are levels not accessible to *hoi polloi*, behind a well-defended gateway at which one will be politely but firmly asked one's business. In Christ Church's case the dangers of this pairing of allure and inaccessibility are felt particularly sharply. An educational institution may legitimately police its boundaries, but it's much harder to see why a religious one should do so. Almost everyone, from the dean's wife to the longest-standing of cathedral volunteers, has a tale of exclusion to tell. Christ Church is the Cathedral of the city and Diocese of Oxford and as such the first message it would seek to convey is one of welcome: it's not easy to justify gatekeepers and turnstiles in the face of this compelling logic of openness.

On moving to Oxford I felt this particularly keenly. Having worked in a parish with a busy community centre I was used to constant unimpeded traffic between sacred and secular: they weren't so much separate territories as superimposed layers. The folding table on which the Eucharist was celebrated each Thursday was for me the key symbol of this. It multi-tasked as domino board, coffee table and football goal, yet transformed weekly into an altar when dressed in a fair linen cloth. The pristine, walled community of Christ Church felt far removed from this small but real anticipation of the kingdom of heaven.

Now that several years have passed I feel rather differently. What looked for my first few months very much like a gated community now seems something much subtler and richer: a place of profound if not always fully realized hospitality. The many gated communities that have sprung up over the past couple of decades are exclusively for those who live within them. Silently invigilated by CCTV and accessed through automatic steel security gates, they tend to instil a sense of suspicion among inhabitants and neighbours alike. I have come to know a number of these developments in parishes across the country.

They are hard to access, even to the invited guest, and they form a growing nexus of privatized zones where a sense of community is particularly hard to foster. Christ Church bears no resemblance to them at all. Yes, there are CCTV cameras here too, but the screens in the porters' lodge tell the story of a shared space, richly peopled: not just the largest but by far the busiest of Oxford's quadrangles.

Tom Gate opens at 7 a.m. and steadily a trickle of visitors make their way under Christopher Wren's tower and around the quad: a verger opening the cathedral, cleaners clocking in, students on their way back from rowing or a night out, canons, clergy and congregation on their way to Morning Prayer and the Eucharist. The intensity of activity quickly picks up after 8 a.m.: college staff, academics, conference guests; vehicles with laundry and office supplies, scaffolding lorries and post vans. At 10 a.m. the tourists with their selfie sticks stream into the quad. But mingling with them will be other visitors: school groups, parish outings, conference guests. Surprisingly often there are processions of one sort or another, sacred and secular: formally attired for a funeral; in academic dress for graduations and university sermons; with banners to mark the centenary of the Women's Institute; bearing flags to celebrate the ordination of women; once even with East African spears and furs for the memorial service of a Ugandan missionary. At 5.30 p.m. people come in their scores and hundreds to choral evensong; and then, as the day draws to a close, the celebrations begin: student society gatherings, formal hall, receptions at the Deanery or in one of the public rooms, parties in the student common room. Recently, after a particularly lively knees-up, our front door appeared in the *Daily Mail*, the background to an unfortunate incident involving an undergraduate with a home-made flame-thrower. This is no gated community, but a place teeming with a diversity of creatures.

And yet for all this diversity Tom Quad is set apart. Its boundaries are demarcated. It is not private, but neither is it simply a public space. The quad is accessible every day of the year, but not indiscriminately – and therein lies its power. The key to this is Tom Tower and its gate. What looks like an imposingly fortified symbol of power and exclusion is actually a threshold of hospitality. The dual foundation that lies behind it is a special place, but it is not an inaccessible one. Its distinctiveness depends on the maintenance of a boundary between the business of central Oxford and the different business of college and cathedral. The gate is not so much a barrier as a threshold across which people are welcomed, so that when they enter this special place they feel special too.

This struck me most clearly when I invited a speaker from the Oxford Gatehouse homeless project to speak in the cathedral one Sunday evening. Alex had lived in Oxford for more than twenty years, often literally on the streets, but he had never been into Tom Quad before and understandably he shared a good few of the common prejudices about the place. But his reaction on coming in for the first time was both humbling and inspiring. Like most of us, at first he was disoriented – how do you carry yourself in a place like this? – but as he relaxed his delight at being invited in was palpable. Over supper before the service he chatted happily about how great it was to see what was on the other side of those stone walls, how privileged he felt to know them from the inside, how his friends would never believe he'd been dining in a seventeenth-century canonry on Tom Quad. And, interviewed during the service, he chose to reveal that though this was his first time inside Tom Gate, it wasn't actually his first time in Christ Church. In his homeless days he had spent many nights sleeping rough in Christ Church Meadow. The meadow, he assured us, is the best place to spend a summer night in central Oxford. Once you've climbed the iron gate behind the Head of the River pub, Christ Church Meadow gives you security, shelter, peace and plenty of soft places to doss down. Seeing Alex out of the quad that evening, I was overwhelmed by his gratitude. Just as the meadow was a special place for him when he was homeless, so was Tom Quad now: a place that confers dignity on those who enter it.

The Eucharist at Christ Church

If this is true of the time and space of Tom Quad, it is more subtly and intensely true of the cathedral and the worship that takes place there. Both on the larger scale of choral evensong and the smaller scale of the early morning services, those of us who work here witness each day the ways in which worship changes people. In fact it is the quiet daily celebration of the Eucharist in the side chapels of the cathedral that has helped me to appreciate the transformative effect that Christ Church at large has on people. It's not for nothing that *Alice in Wonderland* was written by a Christ Church clergyman. With its rabbit holes disclosing new worlds and potions effecting shifts in size and perception, Lewis Carroll's work is a parodic exaggeration of the transformative power of this place. That power is most obviously at play during daily choral evensong. Admittedly a few in the congregation are baffled or bored by what is offered to God, but many more are touched at unaccustomed depths. Some are able to express their joy and gratitude, others are left literally speechless, a shy smile to the clergy at the door being all that is revealed of what they have encountered. It is more intimately seen in the context of the Eucharist that is celebrated daily at 7.35 a.m. A handful gather in the stillness of the cathedral and the sense of anticipation before the service, of attention during it and appreciation after it is keenly apparent among congregation and clergy alike. "Tis good, Lord, to be here', says J. Armitage Robinson's hymn for the feast of the Transfiguration, and each morning those words are made manifest for a handful of worshippers. Daily, in a corner of the cathedral, Christ Church becomes the mount of transfiguration: a time and place apart, that set the day off on a different course, reoriented towards God, the people of God and the things of God.

That is the ideal. Every week, of course, I also meet people who don't know that Oxford has a cathedral and I wish that Christ Church were more unmissable, like Salisbury or St Paul's; I meet people who perceive Christ Church as a wealthy and distant institution, immured in exclusivity with nothing to say to their lives, and I wish we were more like Sheffield, right in the middle of the mix, working daily with the homeless. But these criticisms and insecurities notwithstanding, I am increasingly convinced that the special way in which Christ Church is set apart is more of a blessing than a curse.

In his recent book, *The World Beyond Your Head: How to Flourish in an Age of Distraction*, Matthew Crawford skilfully exposes the ways in which contemporary western culture is squeezing out all times and spaces that are free from demands on our attention. He sees this crystallized in an airport lounge:

Silence is now offered as a luxury good. In the business-class lounge at Charles de Gaulle airport, what you hear is the occasional tinkling of a spoon against china. There are no advertisements on the walls, and no TVs. This silence, more than any other feature of the space, is what makes it feel genuinely luxurious. When you step inside and the automatic airtight doors whoosh shut behind you, the difference is nearly tactile, like slipping out of haircloth into satin. Your brow unfurrows itself, your neck muscles relax; after 20 minutes you no longer feel exhausted. The *hassle* lifts.

Outside the lounge is the usual airport cacophony. Because we have allowed our attention to be monetized, if you want yours back you're going to have to pay for it.[3]

---

3 Matthew Crawford, *The World Beyond Your Head: How to Flourish in an Age of Distraction* (London: Viking, 2015), p. 12.

Christ Church, like every other church and cathedral, has its failings, but it also has much to offer, notably one of the most beautiful and best maintained ensembles of medieval and early modern architecture in the western world, paired with worship sung by a choir of international standing, all of it freely offered. And I believe that its special charism is that of conferring on people the gift of a time and a space that are free from demands on our attention as consumers. All churches, like public parks, school playing fields and common land, are signs of non-utilitarian grace in a world where productivity and price are paramount. And Christ Church has a unique capacity to act in this way by maintaining the delicate equipoise between distinctiveness and accessibility. Set apart but hospitable, this peculiar place lets the grace of God become apparent in people's lives.

The Eucharist in Handsworth

Contrast this with one of the ways in which the Eucharist is offered in Handsworth. At St Andrew's there are three main times and places for the Eucharist: daily in the beautiful early twentieth-century church, monthly in residential care homes, and weekly in the church's Sports and Community Centre. It's the last of these that I'll focus on.

In a small side room in the St Andrew's Sports and Community Centre nine of us are sitting in a loose circle. We have just shared the Eucharist and now wait for a moment in silence, eyes shut, before saying the post-communion prayer together. As at the morning Eucharist in Oxford, the sense of attentive gratitude is unmistakable: this is the still centre at the midst of our varied lives. The harassed teaching assistant, the time-poor grandmother, the time-rich elderly widower whose day holds little other chance of fellowship, have come here to find solace, calm, company. Perhaps above all they have come to devote their attention to something bigger than themselves and their daily routines, something that they encounter with unique intensity in this half-hour of worship that, in glorifying God, also dignifies them:

> By the mystery of this water and wine may we come to share in the divinity of Christ who humbled himself to share in our humanity.

And then in barges Reggie. He doesn't come quietly through the corridor like everyone else; he comes through the fire exit, and as the door opens its seal makes an ear-splitting sucking sound on the metal frame. There's no chair free near the door, so, a little worse for wear at 10.30 in the morning, he totters across the room towards me behind the makeshift altar. He knows what we've been doing – giving out the bread and wine. Fortunately I've left some of the hosts unconsumed for reservation, so I am able to offer him the body of Christ. I try to leave it at that, but Reggie is wise to my subterfuge: 'What about that, Father?' he says, jabbing at the chalice. I might have guessed: slurping at the cup is the highlight of the liturgy for Reggie. But I've already rinsed the chalice: can I really consecrate more wine when I've got to dash to a funeral in a few minutes' time? So, in one of the improvisations that characterize parish ministry, I put aside theological scruples, pour some unconsecrated wine into the chalice and offer it to Reggie, trusting that he has met Christ properly in this act of *ad hoc* eucharistic hospitality.

This scene isn't a weekly event, but ones like it were and are part and parcel of ministry in Handsworth and countless parishes across the Church of England. The Saturday *Guardian* has a weekly column called 'What I'm really thinking', in which people in different careers anonymously give voice to the thoughts they cannot usually express: teachers tell home truths about their students, IT support technicians reveal the staggering incompetence of their clients. But what I'm really thinking when Reggie appears at the Eucharist is hard to articulate. Of course my heart sinks: not again, I think, the dignity of our worship interrupted, as I calculate the time I'll have to invest carefully coaxing him out of the room so that we can lock up. But equally I've been a priest long enough to know that this is the real thing: Reggie's arrival is at least in some sense the arrival of Christ at the Eucharist, even, or perhaps especially, when he arrives late and just as communion is being shared.

Liturgical interruptions such as this one are not lightly to be dismissed. Frustrating though they always are, in my experience they are also manifestations of grace. In the letter to the Hebrews we meet King Melchizedek of Salem, the strange visitor whom Abram encounters in the fourteenth chapter of Genesis. Melchizedek strides unannounced into the Genesis narrative and, uninvited, he blesses Abram. As the writer to the Hebrews elucidates, Melchizedek is an entirely unknown quantity, 'without father, without mother, without genealogy, having neither beginning of days nor end of life, but resembling the Son of God' (Heb. 7.3). He arrives without warning, brings God's blessing, and leaves never to be seen again. Of course it's too neat to identify Melchizedek and Reggie. Reggie never vouchsafed anything of his genealogy, but we certainly saw him again. And yet his discomfiting arrival was and is a blessing: a sign that the Eucharist is not our rite but Christ's, nor our right but a gift for all.

> Deliver us from the presumption of coming to this table for solace only, and not for strength; for pardon only, and not for renewal. Let the grace of this Holy Communion make us one body, one spirit in Christ, that we may worthily serve the world in his name.[4]

Admittedly such arrivals have to be the exception, because it is beyond the capacity of the average parish or congregation to cope with the multiple or frequent advent of either Reggie or Melchizedek into their worship. But the undefended openness of the liturgy as celebrated in the St Andrew's Sports and

---

4 Eucharistic Prayer C, The Holy Eucharist: Rite II, *Book of Common Prayer of the Episcopal Church of the United States of America*, p. 372.

Community Centre – and the fact that it is possible for Reggie to gain unimpeded access to the celebration of the Eucharist – speak powerfully of the quality of welcome and hospitality for which this and many other urban parishes are known:

> Come to this table, not because you must but because you may, not because you are strong but because you are weak.
> Come not because any goodness of your own gives you the right to come, but because you need mercy and help.
> Come because you love the Lord a little and would like to love him more.
> Come, because he loved you and gave himself for you.
> Come and meet the risen Christ, for we are his body.[5]

Unfolding the mystery

The differences between the weekday celebration of the Eucharist in Christ Church and in Handsworth will be clear. One in the near silence of a secluded chapel at dawn, under the expansive canopy of a Gothic stone vault; the other on the carpet tiles of a faintly shabby side room at an urban crossroads, accompanied by the constant rumble of the Outer Circle bus route. One in the inner sanctum of a famous institution under royal patronage, accessed via one of the jewels in Oxford's architectural crown; the other entered off the street in a run-of-the-mill community centre. But what is also clear is that in these two contrasting locations 'a small group of people are [gathered] to do the most important thing in their lives'.[6] What is being encountered, offered and shared is transformative: commemorating the past, anticipating the future and, perhaps above all, attending to the present.

---

5 Christopher J. Ellis and Myra Blyth, *Gathering for Worship* (London: Canterbury Press, 2005), p. 14.

6 Stanley Hauerwas and Samuel Wells, *The Blackwell Companion to Christian Ethics* (Oxford: Blackwell, 2014), p. 11.

As an ordinand, I remember being struck by a prayer inscribed in wood on the sacristy wall of a parish church in which I was on placement: 'Priest of God: celebrate this mass as if it were your first mass, your last mass and your only mass.' For me, this was and is too much. No celebration of the Eucharist is perfect. For president and member of the congregation alike, there are always flaws and distractions, sins of omission and commission. In every Eucharist the body of Christ is made manifest, but also revealed to be, as yet, incompletely realized. But perhaps that sacristy prayer is right in its call for the undivided attention of the celebrating priest. This act of worship is, here and now, the most important thing in my life. In devoting our attention, as wholeheartedly as possible, to this simple set of words and actions, the time and space we inhabit are reconfigured, and with them we ourselves are reconfigured both in our individual psyches and in our collective *polis*.

The contrast, then, is not between Oxford and Birmingham, between Christ Church and Handsworth, but between the world seen eucharistically and the world seen flat. Wherever it is celebrated the Eucharist brings with it the gift of *anamnesis*, making present. Christ, of course, is made present, but we and our context are made present with him. Christ is made present in a new and specific time and place, revealing not so much *how* but simply *that* we are to serve him here and now. The Eucharist does not compel our attention, but it does invite it. Like the space of Tom Quad, which increasingly strikes me as a horizontal picture frame creatively reshaping the perceptions and self-perceptions of those who pass through it; like Reggie, the unwelcome harbinger of grace who blesses us with his demands, the Eucharist refocuses our attention, and does so with a unique intensity. And this, as Simone Weil saw, is important:

> Something in our soul has a far more violent repugnance for true attention than the flesh has for bodily fatigue. This something is much more closely connected with evil than is the

flesh. That is why every time that we really concentrate our attention, we destroy the evil in ourselves.[7]

Those who come to the Eucharist, wherever it is celebrated, find themselves being drawn to attend to the context in which they are worshipping and to the people among whom they are living. Whether defined anthropologically as participant observers, professionally as reflective practitioners, or ecclesi-ally as theologians and children of God, our participation in this collective act of *anamnesis* invites us into a new, fuller and richer world, that of the Christ we share:

> The point of saying that the Eucharist makes the church is that the body of Christ is not a perduring institution which moves linearly through time, but must be constantly received anew in the Eucharistic action. Christ is not the possession of the Church, but is always being given to the church, which in turn gives Christ away by letting others feed on its own body.[8]

---

7 Simone Weil, 'Reflections on the Right Use of School Studies with a View to the Love of God', in George A. Panichas (ed.), *The Simone Weil Reader* (New York: McKay, 1977), p. 49.

8 Cavanaugh, *Torture and Eucharist*, p. 269.

The Priest Attends to the Word: Parish Poetics

RACHEL MANN

Burnage, Manchester

In the incarnational profundity of the Christian understanding of 'Word', the priest and poet Rachel Mann ponders the divine bonds of our humanity. Through them she discerns the dignity and eloquence of those of her neighbours who, by circumstance or by the dissolutions of time or disease, are bereft of words.

I am in the comfortable sitting room belonging to one of the senior members of my church. Blanche is among the most respected and loved members of our congregation. She first came to St Nick's as a twenty-something, along with her husband Bob. She's now in her eighties. She sang in the choir when the church still had one, and enjoys being involved in flower arranging and coming to church socials. She's known as one of the kindest people in the church. She loves to encourage. Ten years after her husband's death she's found a second wind, enjoying holidays with her children and being very active. And, just a few weeks before this meeting, she had a serious stroke.

Blanche has been undergoing intensive therapy. Mercifully it hasn't had a major impact on her motor function, but her speech has been significantly affected. The building blocks of language are there – prepositions, conjunctions and so on – but word order is a problem and similar-sounding words (homophones/near homophones) are regularly confused. At one point – as we talk about the care she's received – she says, with vehemence and distaste, that her carers 'want me to eat the oak of the egg'. It's amusing and it's also sad; Blanche is alive to both reactions. Amusing because the language substitution – oak for yolk – seems to capture something of the claggyness of overcooked yolks; sad because it indicates her incapacity to inhabit language in a manner most of us take for granted. As we chat she acknowledges – with Blanche's typical fortitude and good humour – that she can't quite connect her thoughts and words in the way she used to. It's not simply that words have absented themselves (names are especially tricky), but that they get mixed up. Delightful as our chat is, it is exhausting for both of us. She is constantly aware of the slippages in her speech and I feel I am engaged in an act of translation.

In a time when people are living longer and medicine is improving, Blanche's story is a familiar one. When I speak of Blanche I might just as easily speak of Frances. Frances is in her sixties but lives in a nursing home. As a result of a progressive disease, her language has decayed over time. Yet it takes an unusual pattern. For the first two or three words she speaks beautifully and clearly. Then the sense departs. She continues to speak but her sentences become 'noise'. She is aware of this and finds it extremely distressing. When I (or others) visit her we have learned to ask questions that require only 'yes' or 'no' answers.

There are many others who could be mentioned – who, as a result of dementia or a genetic condition and so on – are excluded, sometimes from birth, from the communicative activities of language most of us take for granted. And we take for granted, too, that the ground for our worship, our theology and our liturgy, may stand confidently upon a sophisticated, multi-layered grasp of complex speech; that the words we speak are a primary connection with the Word who spoke all things into being. Yet for some of God's children the simple route between words and the Word appears to be blocked.

In this chapter I want to reflect on how the humanity and subjectivity of people like Blanche and Frances – seemingly compromised by their exile from the primary social bond of language – can not only be cherished and respected by parish communities, but are themselves icons of the Word. In their seeming otherness they are gift. And I want to suggest that one way of understanding this iconography is through the discourse of what might be called 'parish poetics', in which the priest is called not only to understand herself (and others) as 'poet', but to draw attention to the startling ways in which the parish community participates in God's poetic work. This understanding of priestly vocation is predicated on a kind of gentleness, attentive rigour and respect for otherness that is characteristic of the best poetry. It is a patient work of being attentive to the rhythms and patterns of lives and relationships, and the forms our common life takes. The beauty and fragility of this understanding of ministry rests on respecting the otherness, integrity and difference between persons, an integrity and difference represented in the very nature of the Trinitarian Godhead. This is ministry as a kind of poetic *praxis*, and it is an act of attention.

I'm not suggesting that priests need to take up their pens and start writing sonnets (although as a poet in the traditional sense I don't think that would be such a terrible thing). The craft of poetry is always intentional. It is an act of making, on the same basis as writing a concerto or a rock song or sculpting a statue. Indeed, etymologically, 'poetry' derives from the Greek for making and creating new meanings – *poiesis*. In drawing attention to the poetic dimensions of ministry, I do not want to belittle or evade the skilled and hard-won craft of the formal poet. *Poiesis* is not simply a matter of being struck by 'a muse' or expressing one's feelings and ideas in a versified manner. Not all of us language-users are poets. To become a poet is to engage in disciplined and disciplining practices. Yet it strikes me that, nonetheless, all of us (and perhaps especially priests) contribute not only in rehearsing established meaning but in participating in the creation of divine meaning. One horizon of being human is to participate in God's *poiesis*.

It is not surprising that poets, trained in the disciplines of language, help us unlock how we participate in this creativity; but it's striking how consistently the ideas that poets have about the craft of poetry make a formal space for something wilder, less clearly under the intentional control of the practitioner. Classical theorists called it *furor*, 'frenzy'; their Christian inheritors renamed it *inspiration*, the breathing of the divine breath into the expressive utterance of God's creatures.

The poet and critic Glyn Maxwell offers a suggestive speculation for the origin of poetry, indeed for all art. He argues that as our ancestors left the trees and began to spread across the African plains and savannahs, they 'looked upon' the world and saw that it was good.[1] They apprehended beauty and were filled with delight. Maxwell is not attempting to articulate a fully fledged aesthetics; rather, as a poet and artist, he wants to acknowledge the simple essence of our creative relationship with the world: as a response to beauty, the beauty of pattern and discerned form.

His point, of course, is a neat annexing of God's delight in surveying creation and seeing that it was good. Yet one may read his words not so much as dethroning God but indicating the way we can participate in creation – as beholders and delighters; as co-creators and makers. Like Wisdom in the famous passage from the eighth chapter of Proverbs, humanity's *poiesis* dances beside God 'like a master worker ... daily his delight, rejoicing before him always, rejoicing in his inhabited world and delighting in the human race' (Prov. 8.30–31). At least one great poet, John Milton, finds in that passage a powerful metaphor for the actions of the Spirit, for the co-creation of all things by the Son who would dwell with humanity as frail flesh, and for an elision between the divine breath and human acts of poetic making (*Paradise Lost*, VII.7–12).

---

1 Glyn Maxwell, *On Poetry* (Cambridge, MA: Harvard University Press, 2013).

John's Gospel opens with a deliberate echo of the creative utterance that brings all things into being in the Book of Genesis: 'In the beginning God created the heaven and the earth.' John's echo, 'In the beginning was the Word,' has 'Word ...' become the substitute noun for the whole universe: 'the heavens and the earth'. One does not need to be a philosopher of language or a literary theorist to understand that one fundamental way in which humans participate in creation as makers and co-creators is through and in language. Words construct and structure us as we construct and structure words. The well-spring of our making is language and – theologically, at least – John's bold substitution can be read as indicating a divine foundation for that activity. The Word – which apprehends the world, speaks, writes and makes it – prevenes our own making.

As a maker of poems I am conscious, in my writing, that I'm seeking to make something new – in the sense of 'fresh', in the very least – which re-creates an original delight at beholding the world's wonder. Poets clearly do that in very specific ways, but the theological vision of poetics I am gesturing towards is predicated on the idea that the beauty of the Word – the Divine that not only beholds but has dwelt within the world – is not the preserve of an elite. It is that to which we are all called and in which we all participate. John's profound sentence also places the human body, the incarnate God, in the place of all that is, has ever been, and will ever be made.

And why 'the parish'? In one sense this is an arbitrary matter: a historic way the Church of England has chosen to order itself, and thus contingent. Yet 'the parish' is fundamental to our church's self-understanding. To be human is to be located. Or perhaps better: to be human is to have to negotiate what it means to be both located and dislocated – to have a sense of place and also to negotiate the shifting realities of being human and Christian, negotiating the pressures of change and of transformation, baptized into death and into resurrection.

Writing specifically about women's relationship with poetry, Yopie Prins and Maeera Shreiber make a helpful general observation about the etymology of the verb 'to dwell'. They remind us that the notion of 'dwelling' gestures towards 'a process of perpetual displacement, [reclaiming] the wayward etymology of "dwelling" not as a hypothetical house to inhabit but as a verb that also means to go astray, leading us away and unpredictably elsewhere'.[2] Insofar as the Church of England remains a parochial community, how we participate and dwell in God's poetics remains – for the most part – a parochial matter. Yet, if the poetic Word's 'dwelling' in the world is contextual, it is also, by its very nature, both a place of habitation and a place from which we creatively 'go astray'. The 'going astray' is not a metaphor for immorality – rather it is what leads us into the new. It is in our departures, our alienations from established meanings, practices and ideas as much as in our traditions that we are faithful to the Word's poetic indwelling.

Theologically, then, Jesus Christ as the incarnated Word of God – fully human, fully divine – represents the definitive reconciliation point between the material and the divine. God's making or *poiesis* is not to be reduced to the initial creation and ongoing sustaining of the world; Christ acts as an icon of remaking and re-creating the world. The Word is before the world, but also participates in the world's redeeming. 'And the Word was made flesh, and dwelt among us' (John 1.14). God's fundamental *poiesis* indwells the world and remakes it.

In our participation in Christ – in Church, in Eucharist, as part of the Body – we participate in that creating and our material reality is transformed. 'Dwelling' with and in God is both a recapitulation of the world and a going 'astray', going into the wilderness, a wandering from ready-made meanings. But if that is our vocation in community, it is specifically central to that ministry which gathers up and represents those things

---

2 Yopie Prins and Maeera Shreiber, *Dwelling in Possibility: Women Poets and Critics on Poetry, Reading Women Writing* (Ithaca, NY and London: Cornell University Press, 1997). In Old English 'dwellen' means 'to lead astray', developing into 'tarry, stay in place' in Middle English.

that together make the Church – the priesthood. For even if we abstract the dimensions of the work of priesthood (forgiveness, reconciliation, and so on), it is first an incarnated matter. It is enfleshed, located and dwelt within. Incarnated priesthood comprises the set of practices and ways of being that might be said to make up the *habitus* of ministry. Participating in the poetic – God's making with our collective making – is part of this proper *habitus*. It draws us deeper into relationship with God, the ecclesial community and the world.

Perhaps this sounds a bit abstract. I'd like now to consider how this kind of poetic picture might fruitfully be enacted in one's priestly dwelling in the life of a parish, and specifically to serving someone like Blanche. However, in order to do that, I offer first what I take to be one conventional reading of Blanche's 'oak of the egg' statement (and others like it) in the context of pastoral ministry. I think one entirely reasonable way of understanding Blanche's linguistic and social situation is to pathologize it. Such an understanding reads Blanche's linguistic diversions as a mark of her diminished condition; in this context, our first hope and prayer is that she gets back to 'normal'.

This – let's be clear – is not an unreasonable hope in the ordinary run of things, in the *habitus* of ministry. It was certainly what her family hoped for, for a long time. As her parish priest, I think I shared this hope. Her friends did too. Despite the fact that Blanche didn't feel especially distressed by her verbal playfulness, we wanted her to be able to participate in the more conventional language games the rest of us took for granted. She had speech therapy in order to help her do so. Our knowledge that before her stroke she found such games natural and easy only added to our distress.

However, this reading of Blanche's situation had a significant impact on the incarnated pastoral ministry that I (along with others) was tempted to offer. Blanche's linguistic detours had to be seen as failures and breakdowns. Blanche's speech was understood as a kind of failure of communication, a mismatch between word and thought. She was no longer able to use words to express the meaning she wanted to. She was 'malfunctioning'.

This way of thinking forced Blanche into a kind of passivity, which becomes interesting when placed in the context of how the church community expressed their love and care. I think there was a tendency on the part of the congregation (and indeed myself) to see God as mediated primarily through what was done *for* her: through a kind of 'palliative' care I (along with others) gave her and her family. My 'palliative' care was demonstrated partly in my offering of the sacraments and prayer to Blanche. It was also shown in the simple act of visiting and speaking with her and her family. It was so easy to make Blanche a simple receiver of a reasonably well-delivered and certainly well-intentioned pastoral care that could not allow her to be an active participant.

Once it became clear that Blanche wasn't going to get better, I think this situation was made worse. We were in a 'holding pattern', waiting for the next clinical incident. The aim of the pastoral care was primarily – and arguably rightly – to make Blanche comfortable and, as significantly, to help her family and friends cope with the anxiety and stress of seeing Blanche as 'other' than we were used to, other than she should be.

I am not for one moment suggesting that such 'pastoral' or 'palliative' care was inappropriate. For someone in Blanche's (or Frances') situation – mostly housebound, often exhausted, often struggling with multiple health problems – practical care is Christ's work. To acknowledge, as I think all of us (including Blanche) did, that Blanche was ill and not quite her 'full self' was, in all sorts of ways, sensible. We all had to find ways to acknowledge and accept Blanche's material reality as an embodied person whose ability to participate in community life – of which spoken and written language is part – had been massively compromised by stroke. This process, for Blanche and perhaps most especially her family, was constructed around a sense of profound loss and grief. Blanche was still 'Mum', but

– as evidenced by their tears and anxiety – not quite the mum they'd always known.

But Blanche was not a passive receiver of the sacrament of the Eucharist. My initial theological sketch of 'parish poetics' reminds us of the fundamental significance of the body and blood of Christ, of Eucharist, as a place where Blanche continued in full creative or poetic communion and communication with God and with the Church. In this sense her home communions were not pastoral gifts but shared acts of making. The Eucharist offers one way of understanding the centrality of God's poetics in the work of salvation. Certainly, Blanche's participation in home communion services was a place of encounter with and participation in God's community. In receiving the host, Blanche was no mere passive recipient, but an active participant in God's work of re-creation and remaking of a compromised and incomplete world. Indeed, our very talk of 'communicating' the host indicates that communication – in its original sense of 'sharing' – is at the centre of eucharistic theology and of God's poetics. The abundant 'sharing' of God's very being in the Eucharist is a place of encounter in which – however inarticulately – we share our being in response.

When St John makes his extraordinary poetic gesture at the outset of the Fourth Gospel, he states God's fundamental *poiesis*, his fleshly dwelling place as both vulnerable to damage and the creator of all meaning. In our participation in the Eucharist – in receiving the Word made flesh as part of the body of Christ – we participate in that act of creation. Our material reality, which is itself always incomplete and may be deeply damaged, is placed in a context of God's transformation. All are 'wretched, pitiable, poor, blind, and naked' before God; yet 'if you hear my voice and open the door, I will come in to you and eat with you, and you with me' (Rev. 3.17, 20).

Our participation is no mere passive matter, as if the host were understood as somehow pharmaceutical, in our modern positivistic sense, there to act on a diseased section of the body. The Eucharist is a place where we dwell with God and encounter him; and in that encounter we bring our incompleteness, the potentiality of our deepest longings, needs and desires. Even if we cannot articulate the shape and nature of these longings, the Holy Spirit 'utters' them in the depths of our hearts; they are our desires for wholeness, union and rest in God. In short, we bring our selves, and that portion of God's creativity held in each self, in relation with the Christian community. St Augustine says that the soul knows no rest till it finds itself in God. Our search for union is a hunger to complete our relationship in and with God. The Eucharist is a 'dwelling' with and in God. It brings together God's work of creative salvation and an invitation to us (as signalled at the end of our eucharistic liturgies) to be 'sent out' to live and work in the world as participant co-creators with the *poiesis* of God in the world.

It would be disrespecting Blanche's material, lived reality to ignore the ways in which she was dealing with a situation generated by a medical condition, by physical damage. However, I suggest that Blanche's humanity should not therefore be seen as damaged. She is not someone whose subjectivity and meaning has been impaired because she can no longer play language games predicated on clarity and conventional discourse. Rather, she remains an active locus for *poiesis*, her own and God's. She remains a person who contributes actively to expanding our understandings of meaning and language. God's intention and purposes are being played out not only in but with her. Blanche, in this picture, is less a victim and more a person who can reveal news. She is a gift – someone who in her otherness discloses the dance of meaning between the human and the divine.

To claim that any person is gift is to state the obvious. God's children are all valued and honoured in God's kingdom. The incarnated human reality can be trickier. I am alert to my own sense of frustration and exhaustion when in the company of a person like Frances who through no fault of her own cannot readily participate in the language games I take for granted.

I feel ashamed to admit that. But, in the face of busy-ness, exhaustion and my own inadequacy as a priest and human being, I'm alert to how easy it is to say things like, 'Well, we'll get this home communion or pastoral visit done quickly,' or on a Sunday make the decision to spend time with people who are 'more like me' rather than seek out the person I struggle with, and so on. Of course, I think there is too much clerical guilt and shame and priests often need to learn to be kinder to themselves. However, as priests of God we are being invited to embody God's very character and as parish priests to do so in an utterly located manner. (When language has gone altogether – leaving only the pressure of a hand held, a forehead touched – it can be easier than when the unpredictably assigned blocks of language are still in play.)

So this further horizon of God's poetics that parish priests are invited to embody might be characterized as a poet's quality of attention. With Maxwell, let's speculate that the origin of the poet lies in a kind of beholding – of beauty, wonder and glory. It is grounded in delight. In a Christian context, one might characterize that as grounded in God's delight and beholding, in *poiesis*: 'And God saw every thing that he had made, and, behold, it was very good. And the evening and the morning were the sixth day' (Gen. 1.31).

As priests dwelling in parishes – located, incarnated, in relationship – we cannot treat this alertness to God's gift as an optional extra. Indeed, one dimension of the character of priesthood, rehearsed at all ordinations by the bishop, is the call to be one who watches for divine signs. In the days when I helped prepare deacons for priesthood this was the characteristic of priestly ministry that most were indifferent about. They were drawn to the pastoral or the proclamatory or presidential, not the injunction 'to watch for the signs of God's new creation'. Yet perhaps the willingness to be still, be alert and behold the *poiesis* of God in the lives of others, perhaps precisely in those situations that are most uncomfortable and troubling, is the foundation of our pastoral call and action.

To return to Blanche one final time. I don't think I'm com-
mending a kind of poetic 'alertness' to Blanche (or someone in
her position) as a way of making her or oneself or anyone else
'feel better' about a terrible situation. As if one might exclaim,
somewhat patronizingly, 'Oh look, Blanche has said something unexpected because of her linguistic difficulties, and isn't
that beautiful!' Certainly, Blanche's often wondrous linguistic
detours, of which 'the oak of the egg' is a prime example, do
represent something of the magic of language, and being alert
to a person's idiosyncratic use of words is no sin. However,
I want to suggest something more fundamental: that, given
God's poetic work in the world and our relation to it, all and
any utterance, however apparently random, may be the very
starting point for the illumination of that divine poetry.

This may be demonstrated in many different ways. A person's inability (or even refusal) to play the kind of conventional
language and social 'games' most of us take for granted may
be the point of revelation or encounter with God's otherness,
strangeness or quirkiness. The material reality – indeed, glory –
of those who do not fit easy patterns of the normative may be
the precise moment that our easy categories of the human and
the divine are disrupted. Their 'originality' (with all its resonances of 'origin' and 'source' of meaning) may be the locus of
revelation; and it behoves priest and people to be alert to this.
For tempting as it might be to claim that the nimblest users
of our complex language structures best reveal the image and
likeness of God, Jesus tells us that the seemingly least and most
insignificant are the greatest in the kingdom of God.

W. H. Auden, in his elegy 'In Memory of W. B. Yeats',
famously says that 'poetry makes nothing happen'. More
brutally, Seamus Heaney suggests, 'The efficacy of poetry is
nil – no lyric ever stopped a tank.' In a time when the Church
seems to be becoming ever more frenetic and driven by the
desire to save the institution from annihilation,[3] the useless play

---

3 A retired clergy friend, with nearly sixty years' worth of experience, recently
quoted a anthropologist colleague's comment: 'When the tribe is dying, the

of the poetic may seem unwelcome and irrelevant. The Church increasingly argues that priests and ministers need to be more functional, practical and engaged with change. Of course practical action is important. Poetry – even by the admission of its most significant practitioners – can give the impression of being an idling cog in the midst of the world. The ushering in of the kingdom and the making of new disciples might indeed be better suited to those who drive evangelistic tanks rather than those who write sonnets. Yet the theological picture above has genuine grip in a parochial context. It is my priestly calling to help the likes of Blanche and her family to see God in the reality they now inhabit. But more than that, I am called to be a person who shows the wider ecclesial community in the parish that Blanche as much as anyone else is the ground of God's incarnation here and now.

The poetic resonances of time spent in the company of Blanche and others have stayed with me. As a poet I'm conscious I'm attuned both to hearing the music in language and to listening out for the effect combinations in words and syntax have on meaning. As a poet I also seek to be alert to moments – often utterly ordinary – that act as an invitation to behold God's fearful, beauteous work. It is not, however, the special preserve of the trained poet; I suggest that priest and people are likewise called to be attentive to God's creativity, to be participants in the meanings God makes. It is a dimension I suggest priests ignore at great peril.

---

dance gets faster.' One sometimes suspects this applies rather too powerfully to the C of E.

Office: Marriage

CATRIONA LAING

Dulwich, South London

This is a meditation on the richly liminal place of the office of marriage. It considers the complexity of its ecclesiological history and the divided nature of its identity within Anglican theology. Finally, Catriona Laing sees in this breadth and diversity a fruitful ground for grace, for connecting with a vowed commitment to the holy discipline of love in a generous variety of civic and personal circumstances.

Through a gate in a green and tranquil corner of south London, and down a path under a blue summer's sky towards a cloister. Around the cloister are former almshouses now occupied by elderly residents. Ahead lies the place – old stone and a stout steeple, neat stained glass windows. And there, straight in front of you: the broad wooden door, open to show a glimpse of the congregation inside. A deep breath. After a year of planning and fretting, it is time.

For those who wanted a very English wedding, the little seventeenth-century chapel in the parish where I served my curacy was as idyllic as things get in London. Twinned with a larger, modern church building up the road, it was a magnet for those seeking to conjure up the romanticized nuptials of countless novels and films.

Yet the reality of those weddings was always a long distance from the arcadian nature of the venue. The complex lives of the residents of a vast, multicultural European city continually crashed in on the bucolic surroundings of the parish. There were, of course, rules ('qualifying conditions') as to who could be married in this place – originally a school chapel, and now an unusually attractive adjunct to my parish. It thus possessed a magnetizing attraction for multifarious desires and longings. We had divorcé(e)s wishing to marry again; we had pregnant brides, and couples with children who had not quite got round to getting married yet, because 'other things got in the way'. We had people who had married in a civil ceremony and now wanted their marriage blessed in church. And perhaps inevitably we had same-sex couples who were encouraged by the changes in civil marriage law and assumed it might now be possible for them to be married in church – or at least to have their marriage blessed by the Church.

Few of these people were frequent attendees at the parish on Sunday. They often did not see marriage as an expression of Christian faith in any obvious way. But they did want to be married in church – and not only because of the evocative setting. They sought us out, to be sure, on the understanding that they had a right to be married in their parish church, regardless of their Christian commitment or active membership of the Church. And yet there was, underlying their *desire* to be married in church, a palpable yearning for a transformative moment – some sort of transcendent validation. For me, it spoke to the sacramental nature of marriage, albeit only very intuitively understood. These couples were seeking some sort of supernatural *change* – in their relationship, first, but also in the community of friends and family surrounding them.

In helping them seek that change, I as the priest invariably found myself on the confusing border between the sacred and the civic, the supernatural and the mundane. In an established church in this (supposedly) 'secularized' country, such double-faced liminality is not unfamiliar or unexpected; and other chapters in this book expose and discuss what it is to be poised between the things of this world and the things of the kingdom of heaven. But one might argue, as this chapter will now chart, that marriage is the *supreme* locus of display, in today's Church of England, of its current spiritual anxiety and conflicted theological identity. For not only is the Church not unified in its own core theology of marriage, it is equally strained by the conflicting propulsions between spiritual integrity and financial (or missional) opportunity. There are poignancies and paradoxes to be acknowledged here; but the picture is not all dark. Marriage ceremonies in the chapel I have already described often filled me with worry and dread in advance of them; but almost always grace shone unexpectedly through in the event itself.

Ask any Church of England priest what the Church's position is on remarriage in church after divorce, or sex before marriage, or marriage when children have already been born, or same-sex marriage, and you will get a wide range of answers. This is deeply confusing for all concerned, and often actively distressing pastorally. It is not that the Church does not have 'official' answers to all these issues, once one has refreshed one's memory of the 'canons' and learned how to make one's way around the relevant materials on the Church of England website. Yet the fact is that clergy are still widely divergent in their interpretations, and even encouraged to be so on some issues (it is, for instance, a matter of the individual priest's 'conscience' whether to remarry divorcé(e)s, and if so, which ones). The doors of the church will be thrown open in welcome to all those couples by some parish priests, to some of them by others, and to none of the above by still others; and let us not pretend that financial issues are not relevant here, especially in some struggling parishes where fees for weddings are much needed. So this is a muddling experience for those of us who consider ourselves theologically reflective members and ministers of the Church, let alone for those who are 'visiting' and 'enquiring'. Some examples from my own pastoral experience may be illuminating.

Halfway through my curacy Laura and Karel contacted the parish because they wanted to get married. Laura's grandmother Alice, now in her nineties and suffering dementia, had been an active member of the church for many years. I took her Holy Communion on a regular basis and she always greeted me with a warm smile and a kiss, saying how pleased she was to see me; she then proceeded, each time, to ask me once more who I was. Her husband Ted was not a churchgoer, but he was deeply grateful to the church for the support and love we showed his wife. Laura's father had died when she was young and her mother had not been able to take care of her; so her grandparents had stepped in.

Ted and Alice were enormously proud of Laura. She had a high-powered career in the media and they were delighted that she and Karel were going to be married. Karel was from Croatia and they had met through work. Laura had been through a lot as a child and suffered a great deal because of her parents' complicated lives. Now she had met Karel and she was ready to make the transition from girlfriend to wife with a man who made her feel safe and secure and who wanted to give himself entirely to her. Once we had established that there were no complicated immigration issues for Karel and that the reasons for his divorce from his first marriage were not an impediment to remarriage in church, we were ready to start planning their big day and preparing for their married life ahead.

Neither Laura nor Karel was a committed Christian. Like many in this country today they described themselves as 'spiritual', but they did not want to constrain that sensibility towards any one kind of religion or religious institution. Nonetheless, through her grandparents Laura felt a strong emotional attachment to our church and parish, so there was no question: the pretty chapel would be the place for their wedding.

The day dawned. The drizzle of the morning stopped just in time for Laura to step out of the vintage car her grandfather had borrowed to surprise her. She took his arm, steadying him as she went. He was a little bit wobbly, having determined to walk with a cane rather than his usual Zimmer frame. Laura wore a beautiful 1920s dress, and her bridesmaids looked as if they had stepped out of the latest designer vintage wedding photo shoot. The chapel was completely packed, with media luvvies oozing style and somewhat reluctant to remove their sunglasses, despite the dark chapel and the cloudy skies outside. I wondered whether they might have been more comfortable in a warehouse wedding venue such as one finds in north London – with distressed brick and soulful music on the guitar. In front of the friends sat Karel's family, who had travelled from Croatia the previous week. His father wore a white suit with white leather shoes that reminded me of Elvis, and he beamed from ear to ear throughout the service. They spoke no English, but Laura had gone to the trouble of translating the key parts of the liturgy, so that they could follow along.

There was so much London life with all its colour and diversity and energy in this wedding. We had European immigrants who had moved to the UK in the last ten years and were making their lives here, and their families who had come over for the occasion. We had famous people and randoms who had popped in to have a look at the chapel, which is one of the top tourist attractions in the area. And we had members of the parish who liked to come to weddings where there was a connection with the church. I took a deep breath and prayed that our *Common Worship* marriage service would somehow hold together the glitz and the glamour, the foreign and the quintessentially English, the old and the young, and the secular and the sacred, because I knew Laura and Karel wanted all of it.

It worked. Somehow the whole service evoked beauty and hope. The sense of new beginning was palpable. Past hurt and brokenness in the lives of both partners had been relinquished, and through their marriage service Laura and Karel articulated the transformation they were experiencing as they looked forward to becoming more the persons they felt called to be by virtue of being bound to one another.

But if I had stopped to ask almost anyone in the congregation that day what it was about the service that felt explicitly 'Christian', I am not sure they would have been able to tell me. In circumstances such as these the priest's sense of satisfaction at a marriage joyfully solemnized after months of complex preparation is severely tempered by unresolved theological dilemmas. If Christian marriage *is* a sacrament (a position that has not been upheld consistently in the Anglican tradition), what can be its 'inward and spiritual meaning' for those who do not even subscribe to basic Christian doctrinal tenets? And what then precisely is the *theological* role of the priest in such circumstances as I have described?

My perplexity at these issues during my curacy intensified as other 'non-standard' cases multiplied; indeed, I began to see that 'non-standard' was something more like the 'new normal'. Colin and Tanya's marriage, for instance, shared with Karel and Laura's the motivating idea of a fresh start. Colin and Tanya each had children from previous relationships. They were both south Londoners born and bred. Colin was a decorator and had fond memories of the church, having sung in the choir as a boy and attended scout meetings in the parish hall. Tanya had spent the last eight years raising her three children from a previous relationship. At our second meeting Colin told me that they had just discovered that Tanya was pregnant with their child. More than ever they now felt ready to get married; they told me they wanted to start this new phase of their relationship in a special way. After various setbacks concerning the reception venue, the photographer and the dress (which was modelled on a British design but had been shipped from the Philippines, and somewhere along the line the need for a maternity dress had been lost in translation), this was another wedding memorable for its distinctiveness and joy. At eight months pregnant Tanya was a beautiful bride and their other children were the bridesmaids, page boys and best man. Colin and Tanya certainly did not present the tidy picture of 'Christian' marriage, but the service was nonetheless palpably full of love and grace. Above all, the couple wanted to bring all the aspects of their complicated lives into the Church (including the baby very obviously soon to be born) to be celebrated, blessed and sanctified for their next chapter together. And should not the Church of England more obviously support and sustain this intention than not? Once again I tucked away my continuing theological questions for the sake of this wholly laudable commitment to social 'glue'.

A further example showed me that even practising members of my congregation were now, under the new societal conventions, just as likely to leave marriage for 'later'. Like so many of their friends who had bought their first house and then had children, marriage was not the default option for Becky and James. 'Weddings are so expensive, we just haven't got around to it,' they would tell me when first enquiring about marrying in the chapel. Where James and Becky did differ from their friends was that they bucked the 'not committed members of the church' trend. Indeed, they were at church in our parish most Sundays. Their children, who had been through Children's Church, were now making their way up through the Sunday school groups and hoping to join the choir before long. And they had an extra connection with the church because they had managed to acquire one of the highly sought-after places at the Church of England infants' school in the parish. But Becky and James were also seeking a particular renewal and commitment, along with an act of thanksgiving.

For they had been through a recent trauma: the life-threatening illness of their younger child. The medical condition had been incredibly serious and for a while it was touch and go whether the child would survive the surgery. Thankfully all was now well; they had come through to the other side. For James and Becky, then, a near-disaster such as this was the catalyst to marriage. They felt that their relationship had taken on new meaning as a result of what they had been through together. They had changed; and they wanted to get married to seal the bond that had grown between them through the difficult experience they had shared, and to give thanks for their child's deliverance.

They were excited about planning their wedding. We started to look at the liturgy and talked about what readings they might have. And like nearly every other couple whose wedding I have presided over, they chose chapter 13 of Paul's first letter to the Corinthians. Paul's instructions here are, of course, to the new Christians in Corinth, who were seeking to live as a community and finding it challenging. The letter thus talks about the faith, hope and love that are needed to live well in any such community. In particular Paul lists the attributes of love: love is patient, love is kind, love is not self-seeking, love does not envy, *love never ends* ... For reasons of this last hope alone it is easy to understand why this might be the reading of choice for a wedding, even though its original scriptural context has nothing directly to do with marriage or newly-weds. Notwithstanding its overuse and potentially clichéd tone, I always welcome the choice of this reading since it leaves room for a discussion about how the Church understands that a realistically faithful, hopeful and loving marriage can only take shape, deepen and grow in community. Before the exchange of vows in the *Common Worship* marriage service the priest asks the gathered community: 'Will you the family and friends of *n* and *n* promise to support and uphold them now and in their married life together?' And the people answer, 'We will!'

The transformation sought by these couples I have described happens, then, as part of an act of collective worship and intention. Indeed, one of the most distinctive theological features of Christian marriage compared to civil marriage is the public and *corporate* nature of the Christian service, reliant implicitly on its understanding of the mysterious workings of the 'mystical body' of Christ. The significance of declaring one's love and lifelong commitment to another person in public, asking for grace and blessing to sustain it through the support of the wider body, is the non-negotiable core of Christian marriage – to which, perhaps surprisingly, people such as the couples I have described are deeply drawn. There is then a very real sense in which through the declaration of love, commitment and self-giving, the existing private agreement of perhaps two, five or ten years is transformed into a public vow, which in turn is blessed by God through the priest's action. The Church receives something that does not inherently belong to the Church and makes it sacred, calling God's Holy Spirit to dwell within it. The marriage becomes a sign of divine transformation. It brings the stuff of real life *into* the heart of the Church: the broken relationships as well as the mended ones. Repressing nothing from the past, the Church enables a new covenantal relationship and blesses it, so that the marriage in turn might become a source of flourishing for others.

But what of those who are excluded?

What I have described so far reflects the optimistic and inclusive spirit that drips from the Church of England's webpage, *Your Church Wedding*. The homepage begins: 'marrying in church is personal, meaningful, spiritual and beautiful, *just as you want it to be*'. The tone of the website is that of 'whatever you want, we can make it work for you'. It is not backward in its embrace and welcome to everyone who might wish to be married in the Church of England. There is information on every aspect of the wedding – from wedding preparation and planning the ceremony to how to film your wedding (the 'paparazzi moment' has to be fully indulged), and how to find a match between reception venue and church.

So, had they taken a quick glance at this website, all my anxious couples as so far described might have been reassured that they were likely to pass the test. The website lists the good of marriage: 'good for you, good for the soul, good for families, good for everyone'. On the 'good times' page of the website it declares: 'Marriage is a way of life that brings stability and steadfast love over many years, and this is the kind of love that all of us can support.' The website seems to go to considerable effort to show that all kinds of people might be married in the Church of England. On one level it is an excellent illustration of the encounter between the civic and the sacred – the Church making itself accessible and available for those who are less familiar with its ways: neither previous marriages nor lack of Christian commitment need in principle be a bar, we discover here. Indeed, the website positively assumes that its readers will *not* be churchgoers, only lightly suggesting at one point that in the years following the wedding couples might like to look in to their 'local church' on Mothering Sunday or some other significant anniversary! Note that this sentiment contrasts forcibly with one of the official criteria suggested in the Bishops' Advice for the remarriage of divorced persons in church: their marriage should not, it is underscored there, be a social event involving no serious continuing contact with the Church. Not so the happy laxity of *Your Church Wedding*: apart from a tiny sprinkling of biblical verses and the generic 'wisdom' about the importance of marriage for the stability of society, already noted, we look in vain for a developed or coherent *theology* of marriage; this has to be sought in the substance of the *Common Worship* service itself and in the guiding Canons (B30–B36). Indeed, *Your Church Wedding* is clearly designed as an enticer to those who might otherwise prefer the newer option of a marriage outside either church or registry office ('more churches to choose from than ever before', its link page brags to the consumer; and never a mention of any definitive exclusion). However, the tone of the whole website is disturbingly slick, and there is a glaring absence of invitation or clarity for same-sex couples. The link to the page about same-sex marriages simply states that 'the law prevents ministers of the Church of England from carrying out same-sex marriages, but your local church *can still support you with prayer*'.

What does *this* mean? Now google 'pastoral guidance on same-sex marriage' (if, as a lay person, you are clever enough to figure this out), and a very different story is to be found. The happy, even careless, inclusivity of *Your Church Wedding* contrasts viscerally with the uneasy truce that currently characterizes the Church of England's position on homosexual unions. And this is now very hard to explain to those rejoicing in this country's new validation of their gay orientation and commitment to fidelity. The state may have legalized same-sex marriage (and, of course, some churches in the Anglican Communion do conduct same-sex marriages, to the consternation of the wider Anglican Communion); but the Church of England has not yet made it possible for gay people to express their relationship in terms of covenant, transformation and blessing. Indeed, there is an explicit requirement in the 'Pastoral Guidance' that even 'services of blessing' are not to be countenanced; yet – confusingly enough – it is also stated that pastoral sensitivity must be applied and 'more informal kinds of prayer' are appropriate in the 'light of the circumstances'.

This again leaves a lot of room for interpretation. The hardest thing I have had to do pastorally in the short time that I have been ordained was to tell a gay couple that they could not, after all, have their marriage blessed by the Church. It would be both improper and insensitive to reveal the details of this case, even with names disguised. Suffice it to say that the understanding of 'more informal kinds of prayer' for gay or lesbian couples is already a point of contention, with the issue of the distinction between 'a service of blessing' (clearly forbidden), and a more private meeting with a priest for scriptural meditation, prayer and informal blessing, being hard to quantify. What one priest may initially promise here to a gay couple may come into question with the diocesan authorities before it can even come about. Huge pain and offence is thereby caused, often aborting a much longed for return to church life and worship by the couple concerned. This is a matter of deep pastoral concern and regret.

Here, then, is the hardest *aporia* currently to be faced on the boundary I described at the outset between civil society and Church theology and discipline. The gay marriage issue is, of course, a special case: ostensibly the Bible abominates homosexual relations (though it has no conception of a long-term commitment to homosexual fidelity); and manifestly 'marriage' has until now in the Christian tradition been reserved for a man and a woman. But whereas the Church of England has loosened its discipline on divorce and sex outside (heterosexual) marriage to the point of lassitude in recent years, in the case of homosexual unions, ardently desired ascetic *fidelity* is precisely what it cannot and will not bless.

I wish I had been better prepared for these moral and theological dilemmas over marriage by my seminary training; but the current state of flux means that one is dealing with a constantly moving target (the Pilling Report and further current 'conversations' witness to that turbulence). According to the canons of the Church of England (Canon B30), responsibility to guide a couple preparing for marriage and to help make sense of any practical inconsistencies or difficulties falls directly to the priest:

> It shall be the duty of the minister, when application is made to him for matrimony to be solemnized in the church of which he is the minister, to explain to the two persons who desire to be married the Church's doctrine of marriage as herein set forth, and the need of God's grace in order that they may discharge aright their obligations as married persons.

In order to fulfil this heavy responsibility in *good* 'conscience', and beyond the mere recitation of the rules and guidelines available in the official documents, I have found myself driven back afresh to think through the classic Hookerian authorities of Scripture, reason and tradition as applied to contemporary Christian marriage in the Anglican tradition. This endeavour does not make the Janus position of the priest between civic and ecclesial life any more comfortable; but what at least it has given me is some richer insight into how issues of marriage, sexuality and fidelity have always been ambiguous, complex and even disturbing within the Bible and tradition, and thus always subject (if Hooker is right) to renewed 'rational' testing and reflection. I end this chapter, therefore, with some theological ruminations of my own to which the fractures and difficulties of my recent pastoral experience have led me. It is where I stand at the moment.

Canon B30 states that marriage is for

> the procreation and nurture of children, for the hallowing
> and right direction of the natural instincts and affections, and
> for the mutual society, help and comfort which the one ought
> to have of the other, both in prosperity and adversity.

This classic Anglican (Protestant) understanding of marriage
was, of course, not arrived at without a long winnowing process of change and reflection in the western Christian tradition.
When we probe, first, the complex witness of Scripture (the
prime authority in Hooker's classic triad) we find a bewilder-
ing array of practices and views. The marriages found in the
Old Testament present innumerable accounts of human failure or weakness. God's plan for his people unfolds through
the stories of several barren women (Sarah, Rebekah, Rachel
and Hannah), who become the mothers of the great ancestors
of Israel. Marriage was not necessarily monogamous. Divorce
was permitted (see Deut. 24.1–4), and complicated relationships were negotiated often in response to the need for a male
heir. These accounts describe marriages involving concubines,
polygamous relationships, trickery and deceit; and they remind
us that God can be at work even despite and through these
relationships. Abraham's descendants become signs of God's
promise to his creation. Further, the prophecy of Hosea uses the
image of the adulteress wife to depict Israel's repeated breaking of the covenant with Yahweh as the people abandon their
vows and seek after other gods (Hos. 2.2–13). The prophecy
is called 'The Restoration of Israel' and it speaks of Yahweh's
willingness to restore the covenant every time it seems to have
been broken by Israel. Again and again Yahweh forgives and
restores the relationship with his chosen people. These stories
about marriage and relationships speak to us of the central role
of forgiveness, renewal and commitment that is inherent in
the covenantal promise that marriage bespeaks. They unsettle
any lingering dogmatic fantasy about marital moral rectitude
arrived at without struggle, patience and growth.

Even more unsettling and revelatory, we might say, are Jesus' own particular views and attitudes towards marriage and sexuality. On the one hand his demands are apparently much higher than the Jewish law he inherited – even a lustful glance is adultery (Matt. 5.28), and divorce itself *is* adultery, according to the 'hardest' reading on marriage in the Gospels (see Mark 10.11–12). Yet Jesus, most unusually for a Jew of his time, eschewed marriage himself for the sake of the 'kingdom', and seemingly denied altogether its relevance to the life to come (Mark 12.25). Jesus' own example, in fact, combined both extraordinary ascetic demand and an equally extraordinary compassion for sexual weakness (John 4.4–26; 8.1–11). I find myself constantly forced up against this paradox: to be true to our founder, it seems, the Church must witness to both these dimensions, yet without collapsing into a vapid or careless liberalism as a default third option. The Pauline witness on marriage also complicates the biblical picture, and is no less demanding and ambiguous. On the one hand celibacy is seemingly superior to marriage for Paul, in what he took to be the 'end times' (1 Cor. 7.7); on the other hand, 'it is better to marry than to burn', and women's sexual desires are – remarkably – as important as men's in their rightful need of fulfilment. If the 'deutero-Pauline' literature (see especially Eph. 5.25–33) assumes a more settled and hierarchical vision of marriage than this, it does so on the assumption that '*mutual* submission' (a deeply surprising idea in a patriarchal world) is the rule in a relationship that mirrors Christ's love for the Church.

The tensions inherent in the biblical witness on marriage well explain why in some periods of Christian tradition the Church has seen marriage merely as a compromise for those who are unable to remain celibate, while at other times it has held marriage to be the key image for divine/human faithfulness, a sacred obligation and a profound 'good' for society in terms of stability and procreation. Augustine's influence on both sides of this divergence (his own epic struggles for personal continence and his simultaneous theological justification of the profound 'good of marriage') is the rich but ambiguous inheritance that continues to haunt western reflections on sexuality more than any other. Martin Luther's reappropriation of Augustine's work to argue that marriage was a virtue to which *all* faithful Christians should aspire – necessary for procreation and companionship and as a remedy for concupiscence – is the direct backcloth to the Protestant theology of marriage in the *Book of Common Prayer*. But this was not a 'sacramental' understanding of marriage at its inception; and the idea of the sacramental nature of marriage also has a vexed history, going back only to the later medieval period in Catholic tradition. While the Council of Trent (1545–63) reaffirmed the sacramental nature of marriage, Cranmer's 1549 *Book of Common Prayer* emphasized that marriage was *not* a sacrament and therefore described the rite of marriage simply as 'the solemnization of matrimony'. A ring was given, but not blessed; and there was no full sacramental interpretation associated with the rite, despite the mention of Christ's validating presence at the wedding in Cana (John 2). Only with the growth of the Anglo-Catholic movement in the nineteenth century were there introduced into Anglicanism newly minted catholicizing attitudes towards the 'sacramental' nature of Christian marriage. And evangelical Anglicans still maintain the distinction between 'sacraments of the gospel' (baptism and Eucharist) and the other five recognized in Catholic tradition ('commonly called sacraments').

It is thus when I am confronted pastorally by the complexity, indeed messiness, of the lives of those who seek marriage in the Church of England that I recall something of the equal complexity of this history. And as I find myself each time perched precariously on that difficult threshold between the civic and the sacred, I have to remind myself that the current absence of a united theological agreement about Christian marriage in the Anglican tradition stems also at least in part from the fact that, unlike the other sacraments, marriage is not the *possession* of the Church: it is done by the couple who dare to present themselves for public accountability and divine blessing. And this, of course, reverses the usual direction of travel: the officers who sit on mission and evangelism committees are constantly seeking ways of getting the Church *out* of the church building into public spaces; whereas church weddings offer the opposite. And so we have people who do not usually go to church seeking us out, coming to our door and asking for God's blessing. It feels preciously close to the ministry of Jesus, for in his earthly life people constantly approached him and simply asked for his blessing. In a desperate move to offer a neater explanation of Christian marriage, therefore, there is a risk of reaching for Jesus' demanding words about divorce or Paul's instructions to husbands and wives, lifting them straight out of the New Testament and presenting them as a *simplistic* guide to Christian life practice. In so doing we miss the words God speaks about relationships that are shaped by love, forgiveness, renewal and transformation.

These reflections do not entirely ease my theological conscience; nor do they protect me from the ongoing agony of exercising my priestly 'conscience' on the matter of the remarriage of divorced couples, or from my deep concern about the current scenario for distressed gay and lesbian couples. Nonetheless I must witness again in closing to the invasion of the civic by the sacred that I have experienced in such a tangible way in some church weddings; and this has conjured up a certain sense of holiness, and touched the whole assembled body. It is not there in the form of a list of rules about life practice, but the marriage service highlights the sacramental and transformative nature of marriage when it is enacted in hope by the couple and blessed through the words of the officiating priest. In that sense it is indeed a sign that effects change: 'Pour out your blessing on *n* and *n* in their new life together. Let their love for each other be a seal upon their hearts and a crown upon their heads.' We keep on blessing, because we believe that the Church *can* offer a place of renewal and transformation to many who come and find us.

PART 2

Prayer and Study

The Priest Attends to the School of the Heart 1: Church Schools

FRANCES WARD

St Edmundsbury Cathedral

Frances Ward considers the distinctive ethos of the church school: how it may assist the heart as well as the mind to flourish, how it may nourish spiritual growth as well as competencies; how it may be a training ground for character, resilience and intellectual curiosity rather than for solely marketable skills. Finally, and most important, she considers how our children may learn to imagine and define themselves in terms of their connections – their responsibilities for others, their loves, their communities – rather than in solely individualized labels of identity.

My second child – now a young man of twenty-five – is currently training as a teacher, and applying for posts. He has an interview at a Church of England secondary school coming up shortly. He is at the beginning of what will, I hope, be a long and fulfilling career, teaching young people not only enough to pass their exams but what it means to be a mature adult, with the emotional, intellectual, spiritual and physical resources to cope in an increasingly complex world. Able to form long-term and trusting relationships; able to be good parents; employable and with a fulfilling work/life balance. Able to look beyond their own needs and give of themselves that others may benefit. My son will have, over the next forty years, a key role, directly and indirectly, as a formative influence on the lives of many young people as they grow towards adult personhood.

What lies ahead for him?

Education in Britain today is complex, with political and ideological tensions in play, with much invested, as was ever the case since the concept of 'childhood' emerged in the eighteenth and nineteenth centuries, in children as the future. The formative processes of early years and school are fundamental to the development of the adult person. Much is at stake.

In 2010 Frank Field MP produced *The Foundation Years*, a report commissioned by the then Prime Minister, which recognized that poverty is not merely a material, but also an emotional, social, psychological and cultural phenomenon. Children who are emotionally impoverished, who are poorly attached to parents, struggle to learn in school, to socialize. They are difficult to educate, and often end up in the criminal justice system, or with chronic health problems, or both. Field recommended that the government provide additional resources for the early years of life, from the womb until five years, to enable children to be able to benefit from school. He also recommended that secondary schools educate their pupils in good parenting, and help them to become socially, emotionally, culturally literate so they can form trusting relationships as adults. He spoke of the 'rupturing of a good parenting tradition' over recent decades, and that it should be a priority to reverse this social trend, for the good of society. He was surprised to hear – from teenagers – that they agreed.

Some time ago, I asked to meet a group of 15 year old pupils in one of Birkenhead's most challenged schools ... I asked each of them to list for me which six outcomes they most wanted to gain for themselves from attending school. Their replies both shocked and delighted me. Without exception, all of these young citizens stated that they wanted their school to be a safe place, to help teach them what was involved in building long-term friendships and to equip them with the necessary skills to gain a good job. Most surprisingly, all of the pupils listed ... the wish to be taught how to be good parents.[1]

Field talked afterwards with the head teacher and learned that perhaps ten out of the group of twenty-five had rarely, if ever, known their parent, or parents, to put their needs before their own.

Yet none of these young people judged their parents – they phrased their request as wishing to know how to be good parents. Some of the group were scruffy, their clothes washed less often than those of other children, and apart from school dinners they had no certainty when they would next be fed ... where they would sleep that night ... would they gain entrance when they went home ... they prioritised the need to know how to be good parents, not simply better parents than the ones they had inherited.[2]

This chapter considers the role of Church of England schools in the UK today, the distinctive contribution they can make and how the Church of England minister can enhance that contribution. Church schools have their ideological detractors, but are widely recognized as offering a high standard of education to children and young people that is valued by parents, whether churchgoers or not. I will suggest here that, in a time of change, the Church of England should take the opportunity to become more distinctive in what its church schools offer, drawing on the resources of Christianity, mining the long traditions of reflection on how human personhood is developed and shaped. One of the ways that can happen is through the contribution made by local clergy and lay people to their church school. Behind my thinking is the assumption that education is a formative process that enables habits of the heart, mind, soul

---

1 Frank Field, *The Foundation Years: Preventing Poor Children Becoming Poor Adults*. The report of the Independent Review on Poverty and Life Chances (London: Cabinet Office, 2010), p. 19.

2 *The Foundation Years*, p. 19.

and strength to be established, that in turn enables the person to love God and other people as themselves, so that it becomes second nature to be self-giving, to put the needs of others above one's own, with a commitment to make a better world.

The Great Commandment of Jesus Christ – to love God with heart, mind, soul and strength, and one's neighbour as one-self – will provide the frame for what follows; but first, some clarifications and a little history.

Clarification and a little history

Let me start with a clear assertion: church schools are not faith schools. This may seem an odd thing to say; because, of course, a Church of England school is going to be concerned about faith, for God's sake. But it is important to clarify an import-ant misconception that is often made. A 'faith school' is one that serves a particular faith group, whether Muslim or Jewish or Pentecostal, and will, typically, have an admissions policy that draws children predominantly from that particular faith group. A 'church school', on the other hand, offers education to the children within its catchment community regardless of their religious or denominational background. Church schools will reflect the surrounding community: some are mainly, or even totally, educating Asian-heritage children, for example.

To give a little history, the Church of England's engagement in education dates back to 1811, when the National Society was founded, and the Church of England first promoted 'the education of the poor in the principles of the established church'. By the time of the 1944 Education Act, a large pro-portion of the nation's schools were church owned and run. This act reformed the educational system after the Second World War, primarily to provide secondary education for all children. Church schools became either voluntary-controlled or voluntary-aided: categories that designate two differ-ent levels of local parish and diocesan responsibility for the financial and governance provision, working alongside the local education authority. School worship was made obligatory in all state-maintained schools and religious instruction became obligatory in all schools in accordance with a locally agreed syllabus. During the 1980s and 1990s there was a plethora of Education Acts, and continuing debate about the role of religion in education, which continues at the present time. In an increasingly secular age, the question of the extent to which education should be 'religious' and what that means is never far away from consideration, and has become of particular interest as other faiths have claimed the right to have state-sponsored faith schools.

All this has changed with the recent political support and encouragement for schools to become 'free' of local authority control. Such schools are called either 'free' or 'academies'; the name matters less than the freedom the school has to set its own curriculum and ethos, as part of what are emerging as academy chains. The National Society and Church of England Dioceses are in the process of creating Multi-Academy Trust chains which offer support to those schools that opt for free school status. The Church of England faces a time of real upheaval, which might see its reach through education diminished significantly. A time of threat is also a time of opportunity, though, for Church of England academies will need to promote a distinctive, strong, inclusive ethos to commend themselves in a competitive environment.

So what has made Church of England schools distinctive to date? The culture or ethos of the school, ideally, will have been established by the head teacher and governors, usually with local clergy, and will have embedded particular values to enable children of different faith backgrounds, and none, to feel at home. Sometimes the Christian teaching and virtues have not be explicit, for fear of causing offence, but rather the Christian roots of the school have been evident in a commitment to the needs of the whole child, with recognition of spiritual alongside the emotional, intellectual and physical needs. The local

clergy and lay people usually will play a key role in leading
assemblies, offering teaching and classroom assistance, and
as school governors; and the extent to which Christian stories
and discipleship are emphasized will depend on a number of
factors, not least the extent to which the local church school is
viewed as an opportunity to introduce children to Christianity.

In practice this has meant that there is very little difference
between a church school and a state community school. Indeed,
there are state community schools that have a greater Christian
ethos than the church schools around, because of the influence
of the head teacher, for instance. Some church schools, on the
other hand, can show little evidence of any Christian foundation in their day-to-day routines and practices.

Key questions

I find myself now plunged into key questions about where
the future lies for the Church of England in education. In
Bury St Edmunds, we have recently undergone a Schools
Organisational Review, which has closed the middle schools,
including St James' C of E middle school in the tiny parish that
belongs to the cathedral. We are faced with a real opportunity
to open a new primary academy or free school that will enable
us to develop our musical provision to support the choirs of
St Edmundsbury Cathedral, and enhance the musicality of
children who will go on to the secondary schools in the town.
A decision has recently been made to explore further joining a
new Cathedrals Academy Trust that is currently being set up
to enable cathedral schools to develop their distinctive national
contribution as choir schools. This will mean being at the fore-
front of a new educational era, with all its opportunities and
potential pitfalls. At a time of change, what more might the
Church of England nationally contribute to the education of
children at primary and secondary levels? How might that education, as a formative process of deep significance in a person's

life, shape the adult? What is distinctive about what Christianity brings to this formative process that enhances what it means to be a human person?

This begs an important question about the nature of the human person, one that requires greater clarity, as different conceptions of personhood will emerge in a plural society. I have in mind three assumptions that tend to be made in western secular society today. The first is to value individualism over belonging to community. In educational terms, this can mean that a child will be placed at the centre of her education, as an individualistic atomized 'self', following her own pathway through, seeking self-actualization as the goal. Then, the category of 'identity' is often the dominant way of speaking of oneself. Identity – whether defined on cultural, religious, gender, or sexuality lines – is often the first descriptor that a person will use. Such identity labels can foster a tribal sense of belonging rather than a commitment to humanity as a whole. Faith (as opposed to church) schools can tend in this direction. Third, it is hard not to be caught up into an instrumental or utilitarian mindset that values things and relationships only in terms of how useful or purposeful they are. Western society today tends to be individualistic, tribal and instrumental. We need to ask ourselves, as a society, whether there are other, better ways of being human. I suggest here that Christianity offers wisdom to the question of what enhances human personhood. Based on the narrative of the life and death, the self-giving of Jesus, a Church of England education can offer a pedagogy that has a different philosophical anthropology at its base. The Great Commandment of Jesus Christ in the Gospel of Mark (12.29–31) has it:

'Hear, O Israel, the Lord our God, the Lord is one. Love the Lord your God with all your heart and with all your soul and with all your mind and with all your strength.' The second is this: 'Love your neighbour as yourself.' There is no commandment greater than these.

To take this commandment as an end in itself is to conceive and shape the human person in particular ways.

An end in itself

Education. Is my education useful to me because it will enable me to gain self-fulfilment? Will I get on in life as a result – go to the best university, get a good job? Is education a means to an end? For many, it can be hard to see that education is anything else – and sometimes because such things should be the indirect result anyway. To understand education not instrumentally, but as an end in itself, as worth doing for its own sake, is difficult. But it is important to hold onto this principle. Education is an end in itself. It is for its own sake. In a church school perhaps one can go further and say that education is for God's sake. If seen like this, then church schools can offer the opportunity of an education that shapes the child, and therefore the adult, in particular ways, drawing on the insights of Christian traditions to understand and know what a human person is. As the child grows and develops through school, the rich resources of Christianity – in its narratives, in its worship, in the wisdom gained through centuries of thought and reflection on the Judaeo-Christian Scriptures – can enable children to grow into a maturity of heart, mind, soul and strength, loving their neighbour as themselves. To be individual, not individualistic. Not to belong to a tribe to bolster a fragile sense of identity, but to have character. To do things and treat people as ends, not as means to one's own ends.

How might a more intentional Christian anthropology inform pedagogy and educational practice in the local church school?

To take the Great Commandment as foundational would be to consider the growth of the child towards mature personhood emotionally, intellectually, spiritually and physically, framing that growth and development in relationship with God and neighbour. The intellectual question of whether 'God' is a given in someone's life (theism), or a constant question of doubt (agnosticism), or a definite absence (atheism), would be given its proper place as an ongoing open question that assumes a relationship with 'God' is worth struggling with as the person, child and adult, grows in a continual process of formation. The assumption can be made, and then argued with, about 'God': does 'God' provide an ultimate referent that can be helpful in a number of ways for the person? For example, by providing a moral compass (the Ten Commandments have age-old credibility)? A psychological referent (you are not alone in the world – love is the foundation of all)? A cultural referent (the concept of 'God' has inspired some of the most excellent art, architecture, poetry and music through the ages – it's worth wondering what that inspiration is about)? These are crucial questions to ask and seek answers to, and in the process the child and adult will find themselves formed as a person in conversation with believers and doubters through the ages.

The mandate to 'love your neighbour as yourself' takes one in a more intentional Christian direction, away from the usual moral injunction of the Golden Rule, where all that is expected is that one should treat others as one would wish to be treated. By contrast, to love one's neighbour is much more active. It asks of the person that they commit themselves to the service of others, looking for ways to volunteer to help whenever possible, to care for those in need around, to become engaged in work and careers that enhance the lives of others, taking seriously a vocation to public service and careers like teaching. At heart, loving neighbour as self means leading a life of continued challenge to self-centredness, or self-promotion, or self-interest. So not following a career that is simply about making money becomes important. Going the extra mile when required, in a self-sacrificial way, becomes second nature. It is crucial, of course, that someone embarked on such a life really does love themselves too. Good self-esteem and self-worth are vital if one is to love one's neighbour. Otherwise what really happens is that one's own needs for love dominate in subtle and not-so-subtle ways, to the detriment of self and the others for whom one tries to care.

It would take time and careful exploration with head teacher, teachers and governors, and parents, to develop such thinking into a clear strategy. Such a process in itself would be positive, if undertaken thoughtfully, enabling staff and governors to grow in understanding of what it is that is distinctive about the Christian way of life, and what it means to offer a formative education based upon such a life. With that Great Commandment to help us to think about the child as he or she grows to mature human personhood, let us take each of those areas in turn.

With all your heart

With a husband who is a paediatrician, often our pillow talk takes off in strange directions. He is professionally interested in attachment theory: how one helps parents bring up securely attached babies and young children. Love matters: if a child receives the right attention from earliest days, then the architecture of the brain develops normally, and the child grows into an adult who can form trusting relationships, with emotional maturity. When it goes wrong, as so often it does, the child is difficult to educate, and may end up in the criminal justice system, or with chronic health problems, or both. The latest research in attachment theory by Patricia Crittenden, building on John Bowlby's foundations and Mary Ainsworth's work, brings it together with family systems theory to provide a comprehensive understanding of how poor attachment has trans-generational repercussions. Breaking such cycles is hard, and costly, if tackled through therapeutic care for individuals within their families.

Many schools face increasing issues that result from poor attachment. What can church schools do to minimize the difficulties so that a child is able to be educated – to learn, to socialize, to develop towards an adult maturity that means she or he does not replicate the damage when their own children are born?

An interesting body of literature is emerging from the United States and Canada that may help church schools, both primary and secondary, to equip children and young people to develop the emotional self-awareness and skill required for adult life – to give those Birkenhead teenagers the qualities they were looking for. Paul Tough's book *What Makes Children Succeed* stresses the importance of self-control and the nurturing of resilient character. David Brooks' *The Social Animal* also commends the importance of developing habits of the heart that enable the child to delay immediate self-gratification. Brooks argues that 'people with self-control and self-discipline develop habits and strategies that enable them to perceive the world in productive and far-seeing ways'. Character, he says, 'emerges gradually out of the mysterious interplay ... and ... power of small and repetitive action to rewire the fundamental mechanisms of the brain. Small habits and proper etiquette reinforce certain positive ways of seeing the world.'[3] Habits of the heart, nurturing a sense of character, enable the formation of the child into adulthood in beneficial ways for the individual and for the society to which she or he belongs.

With Crittenden's work, both books are invaluable resources that suggest how education might be more formative of the person's emotional character to prepare them more helpfully for adult life. Self-control is, of course, one of the nine fruits of the Spirit listed in St Paul's letter to the Galatians. Perhaps church schools could do more to focus on those virtues of character as a way of developing a sense of second nature that offers emotional and moral knowledge to resource the challenges of adulthood. N. T. Wright's book *Virtue Reborn* gives an invaluable source for further thinking along these lines.

---

3 David Brooks, *The Social Animal: The Hidden Sources of Love, Character, and Achievement* (New York: Random House, 2011), pp. 150, 154.

Church schools could pioneer such research, bringing together the latest insights with the Christian wisdom of traditions of formative practices that go back to, among others, St Benedict, to St Paul, instilling within children and young people the emotional self-control and ability to put the needs of others, including eventually their own children, above their own gratification.

With all your mind

Habits of the heart; habits of the mind. How do we learn to learn? To think clearly and carefully? Dorothy L. Sayers wrote an essay in the 1940s, *The Lost Tools of Learning*, which takes us back to a different era, but which may offer wisdom into today's complex education world. She looks back to the classical education of the Middle Ages, and the practice of training the mind with necessary tools of learning. She does so, however, with an awareness of child developmental theory as it began with Jean Piaget in the 1930s, and maps that new knowledge onto the old wisdom. It is well worth reading. With limited space here, let us glean what we can.

Sayers argues that a child has three clear stages of development at which they learn. The first, from the very beginning, is an absorbent time, when the child will learn all sorts of things quickly and easily, able to memorize, keen to distinguish different categories of things, often enjoying words for the sound of them, without understanding fully what they mean. Sayers believes that this is the time for the child to learn as much as possible, knowledge that will offer a bedrock that will prove helpful to later stages. The second stage is when the critical faculties start to come into play. The child will enjoy arguing, playing, catching others out. The third stage is when both the knowledge gained in the first stage and the ability to question and argue in the second stage come to fruition in the ability to make a good case, to persuade in a cogent, careful way. Sayers believes that these basic tools of learning are the essential acquisition of a good education which correspond to the classical *trivium* of the past, of grammar, dialectic and rhetoric. This method provides enough for the adult person to think for themselves, not taken in by false propaganda or poor argument. It is a good essay, well written and persuasive; although she is very aware that even in the 1940s her views would be controversial in educational circles. She is keen, for example, that very small children learn Latin, as an awareness of grammar structure from an early age enables the development of a facility with language that becomes more difficult to acquire the older one gets. This begs the question: if her views are valuable today, how might they inform the Church of England in its educational policies, and local church schools as they help children to learn to think?

Interestingly, in my local town the primary schools are beginning to reintroduce Latin. It is making a comeback! Perhaps this might also lead to a greater appreciation of how small children, of primary school age, enjoy learning things off by heart. Sayers emphasizes how much fun it can be, giving the child the sense of a satisfying achievement, when presented in a positive way. Parents and carers can help very small, pre-school children to start to make the connections in their minds: nursery rhymes, simple poetry, multiplication tables, prayers, all can be made a game that helps the child learn, enables the child to gain the first tool of learning. Church mother and toddler groups can with confidence play games that consciously engage the child's natural desire to enjoy words, with a real emphasis on learning things off by heart as a game, as fun. Then when children start to answer back, Sayers identifies this as the dialectic stage, and commends the encouragement of argumentativeness, and the proper learning of how to argue properly, with cogent logic and reason. Any subject can be used to this purpose, including engaging a moral sensibility in exploring motivation, and analysing action. How might a junior church or Messy Church session, or assembly or school RE lesson engage children with their inquisitiveness about faith, about God, about Jesus? Sayers would say that when children have a good knowledge base, their questions in this dialectic stage are absorbed and absorbing, as they grow to have a moral framework. To shape this frame in an explicit Christian way is to emphasize self-giving as part of a community, a sense of character, and doing things for their own sake, or for God's sake.

The rhetorical stage starts to bring learning together. It was perhaps best illustrated by the film *The History Boys*, with its delightful exploration of the pleasure of gaining the tools of learning in order to enjoy the fruits of persuading others. Sayers writes that a certain freedom is demanded that allows the teacher and pupil to range across different disciplines, and develop self-expression on the basis of the foundation laid. She comments: 'Any child who already shows a disposition to specialize should be given his head: for, when the use of the tools has been well and truly learned, it is available for any study whatever.'[4]

One of the places where Sayers' understanding of education as providing the tools of learning can still be seen in practice today is in the training that a cathedral chorister receives. From the age of about seven, a child is gradually introduced to highly sophisticated music, often in foreign or ancient language, and learns such material off by heart, to perform to an extremely high standard. By the time the child has grown through puberty, they have a cultural repertoire that they never forget, that inspires the majority to continue to sing and perform. And because they have learned to perform, many go on into public life. It would be interesting to see how much of this pedagogy that is alive and kicking in Anglican cathedrals in the UK and around the world might be transferable to church schools, so that the tools of learning experienced in song schools are developed in other areas of primary and secondary school education. The local clergy and church, too, might decide to

---

4 Dorothy L. Sayers, *The Lost Tools of Learning* (London: Methuen, 1948), pp. 25–6.

direct resources into encouraging children and young people to make music within the church context, by promoting music and singing in choirs, as a fruitful way of countering the excessive individualism and utilitarian trends that shape many of today's children. In most dioceses, the experience of cathedrals and their music departments is there to be drawn upon.

With all your soul

The Great Commandment differentiates heart, mind, soul and strength as it also holds them together. What does it mean to have a 'soul'? Perhaps something along these lines: a sense of awe and wonder at that which is mysterious, including language, and words that are not immediately understood. A conscience, that enables the person to tell right from wrong, to feel shame when offence has been caused, to be moved to say sorry. An aesthetic sensibility that prompts the person to respond to beauty, or to find in nature and the universe a freshness felt deep down. To have a soul is to begin to understand the height, length, breadth and depth of love as experienced in relationship with other people and with God as the ultimate ground of loving being. How might a church school enable the child to grow in this dimension? As someone who knows how to nurture their spiritual life? Again, enabling certain habits to develop might help.

One of my most formative experiences was a profound sense of awe as I sat out one night under a sky of stars and came to the sudden realization that I was a very small part in the great scheme of things that is the universe. My response to that enormity was a sense of saying 'yes'. I could not say to whom the 'yes' was addressed, but it began, for me, a lifelong exploration into a relationship of love and thankfulness for the gift of life. When one sees one's personhood in these terms, one has a very different understanding of what it means to be human. Life is based on a sense of gift. It becomes much less easy to think in terms of rights. One does, of course, have rights, as our society conceives them, and it is really important that such rights have their place to ensure that justice and opportunity are there for everyone. To base one's understanding of self on gift rather than right means, though, that one will tend to give thanks for what one has rather than forever seek what one does not have. The habit of giving thanks is the beginning.

Closely allied to the word 'gift' is forgiveness. In a world where cycles of revenge and violence can easily become the norm, particularly when the honour of an individual or group is offended, to learn the importance of forgiveness becomes a particular gift that Christianity can offer. To learn to forgive takes time and practice, best begun from one's earliest years.

A sense of gift, and the ability to forgive, based on the knowledge of the presence of love in the world: how might a primary or secondary church school ensure that such values become the bedrock of the culture and sustain the ethos of that school? Stories that illustrate; visiting places that inspire awe and wonder; acts of worship that offer thanks and gratitude that are an essential part of the school day; there will begin habits of the soul that form the child into someone who is able to love, to give and forgive.

With all your strength

Robert Macfarlane, in his book *The Old Ways: A Journey on Foot*, writes this:

> The relationship between thinking and walking is also grained deep into language history, illuminated by perhaps the most wonderful etymology I know. The trail begins with our verb to learn, meaning 'to acquire knowledge'. Moving backwards in language time, we reach the Old English *leornian*, 'to get knowledge, to be cultivated'. From *leornian* the path leads further back, into the fricative thickets of Proto-Germanic,

and to the word *liznojan*, which has a base sense of 'to follow or to find a track' (from the Proto-Indo-European prefix *leis-* meaning 'track'). 'To learn' therefore means at root – at route – 'to follow a track'. Who knew? Not I, and I am most grateful to the etymologist-explorers who uncovered those lost trails connecting 'learning' with 'path-following'.[5]

To learn is to follow a path. It encourages the person to walk. There is an increasing research that indicates that walking is good for us. It enables the person to be strong and healthy, fit and active. It has been beloved of writers: many need to walk in order to think – as Macfarlane is suggesting. Walking can enable psychological health too. In the words of Søren Kierkegaard, the Danish theologian:

> Above all, do not lose your desire to walk. Every day I walk myself into a state of well-being and walk away every illness. I have walked myself into my best thoughts and I know of no thought so burdensome that one cannot walk away from it. If one just keeps on walking, everything will be all right.[6]

Many are concerned about how much time children spend in front of the screen today, and how in one short generation the habit of playing outside has gone. There is a growing literature on the toxicity of childhood, and some wonderful literature that commends not only walking but time spent out of doors generally. The Forest Schools movement actively seeks to commend a re-engagement of children with the natural world, not only for their own fitness and well-being, but also because a sense of good stewardship of the natural environment becomes an increasingly urgent imperative. When children know and

---

5 Robert Macfarlane, *The Old Ways: A Journey on Foot* (London: Penguin, 2013), p. 31.

6 Søren Kierkegaard, letter to Mrs Henriette Kierkegaard, 1847, quoted in Ian Bradley, *Pilgrimage: A Spiritual and Cultural Journey* (Oxford: Lion Hudson, 2009), p. 75.

understand the natural world around them, they begin to
honour and care for it in ways that are not possible in ignorance.
I remember taking two ten-year-old boys, friends of my own
son at the time, on a nature walk, pointing out the difference
between hawthorn and elder, between a baby blackbird and
a starling, and even on one occasion glimpsing a kingfisher;
it took two such outings to turn a couple of rough youngsters
into lads who were sufficiently turned on to the natural world
to lead me to hope that they would continue to engage and
care as they grew into adulthood. It didn't take much. Many
primary schools are reintroducing nature walks and exploration of their local natural places, to discover what wildlife may
be found. Local churches could provide exciting opportunities
to collaborate with church schools to offer local knowledge
and projects, for example in the churchyard, that enhance the
engagement of children with nature. With an underlying understanding that the world around is an evolving created order,
revealing the creative love of God, rich in its diversity, church
schools could do – are doing – much to strengthen the child's
sense of awe and stewardship of the natural world. Physical
well-being and strength of body also result from such engagement with the world outside the classroom.

In conclusion

This chapter has offered some ideas that might enhance the
Christian ethos and culture of church schools by focusing on
the heart, mind, soul and strength of the child. Education is
viewed here not as a means to the end of the self-fulfilment
of a good career, or the self-realization of the individual, or
the self-expression of a particular 'identity'. The goal of education is that the person may grow as a human being who is
able to love, with attention to the other, because she or he has
emotional, intellectual, spiritual and physical well-being and
health.

Loving – whether God is seen as the inspiration of that love or not – with heart, mind, soul and strength gives the child and adult a foundation in life that begins with the formative processes of early childhood and school, and fosters a sense of human personhood marked by the ability to contribute to the society and world around in a life that is shaped by self-giving, forgiveness, love of others, and commitment to public service and to the natural environment. Such a concept of personhood, as the goal of a lifelong education that begins at birth, but is most formed and developed through school, requires a good sense of self-esteem and worth.

> ... they wanted their school to be a safe place, to help teach them what was involved in building long-term friendships and to equip them with the necessary skills to gain a good job. Most surprisingly, all of the pupils listed the wish to be taught how to be good parents.

Self-esteem and worth begin as the growing person looks outwards from self, learning habits of the heart, mind, soul and strength that take one away from self-centredness and the desire for immediate self-gratification, towards the ability to be self-giving, putting the needs of others before one's own. The Great Commandment asks of the human person that she or he love God with heart, mind, soul and strength, and the neighbour as self. To know what it is to base one's life on love, and to express that love with self-giving resilience of character, is to begin to realize a mature human personhood. It is this the teenagers in Birkenhead were seeking of their school education. Church of England schools are well placed to make an even more distinctive contribution to that end.

The Priest Attends to the School of the Heart 2: Parish Theology

VICTORIA JOHNSON

Flixton, Manchester

In this chapter the parish church is re-imagined as a place of profound and lifelong learning, where personal history and the long life of a community meet richly: a place of divine gift and of discipleship; of refuge and sanctuary; of equipping and re-equipping for the responsibilities of sharing and participating in God's sacrificial love.

When you walk into a church, are you walking into a kind of school without even knowing it? Do you expect it to change your mind? Your heart? Your life?

Like thousands of other churches, St Michael's, Flixton is full of history: some remembered, most forgotten. There was probably a small wooden Saxon structure here, but apparently even then it was known as the 'old' church of St Michael. The local history society has talked about the possible Celtic origins of its site, set upon a slight rise and located at the convergence of two rivers, the Irlam and the Mersey.

Today St Michael's is a curiously unified amalgamation of medieval, Georgian, and Victorian rebuilding. Sandstone, wood, whitewash, glass. It's a cosy church – some call it 'the friendly gem' because as soon as you walk in you feel welcome, at home, embraced. In some ways it's too intimate, even exposing. Nothing can be hidden here. It was once a village church in a country parish, with a country parson. Today it has to keep up with suburban values and city life as the metropolis of Manchester reaches into rural Cheshire.

All you do know, when you walk into this church, is that the walls are thick with prayer and you are greeted with quiet; a space is waiting for you to speak to God, or for God to speak to you. You are here because countless generations before you have, in word and deed, handed on belief. In places like this, the faith is kept, the faith is taught.

As I look on glass (mostly eighteenth and nineteenth century) I see tales of resurrections, births, ascensions; of good shepherds, green dragons and warrior angels, speckling the church with dazzling red, blue, green and yellow light.

The churchyard is full of human story. The village fiddler was buried here, and the wife of the standard bearer in the battle of Waterloo, her only claim to fame being her husband's glory. Gravestones tell the stories of family tragedies, child after child lost to disease, sacrifice in both world wars. This little community was touched by the Munich air crash in 1958; the captain of the Busby Babes, Roger Byrne, lived here – in the days when footballers lived in normal houses, not gated millionaire mansions. Crowds lined the cobbled street for his funeral, watching the coffin being carried past the pub next door and into the church.

So much to take in, so much to learn. There is nothing unusual about St Michael's. Every church tells its own story, is a university of lives lived, love shared, faith explored. Churches speak to us. It's amazing what you can learn by standing still in an empty church.

Our churches are not museums. Our present lives also are gathered into these stones; we are books in these libraries of faith. New stories are being written all the time. Last year we had a proposal at the Christmas carol sing-along, and the incident has already become part of parish folklore. A long-awaited baby arrived early for his first Christmas and slept through the Nine Lessons and Carols. At Midnight Mass, a young man with cancer came to receive Holy Communion with his mum. It was a milestone he thought he might not reach. The building is being shaped by the lives of those who enter, and those lives, in some intangible and unmeasurable way, are being shaped by its stones.

I've often reminded the children that the church is made of other stones, which laugh and cry, shout and despair, rejoice and doubt and hope. These stones are flesh. It's a vicar's standard trope: 'the Church is the people', I say. What can we learn from them? Without these people the vibrancy of this place will fade, the building will begin to look shabby and uncared for, it will smell of decay and abandoned prayer. The two churches, of stone and of flesh, are dependent on one another. And yet it's the romantic image of the empty church that haunts the poems of Larkin and Betjeman and Gray. It's the empty church that attracts artists, tourists, pilgrims and school groups who want to learn about the Christian faith.

Walk into this church on a Sunday, and it's a different place, teaching different things. There's hustle and bustle – there's rarely silence before the service, however hard we try. There are comings and goings, there are children darting here and there, there are Zimmer frames and mobility scooters and buggies, there are processions, there is music, there are grumbles and gossip (we're not perfect), laughter and tears. In the prayer corner, candles are lit, petitions are offered to God on Post-it notes. The worship begins. We sing, we hear Scripture, we hear the sermon. I'm always amazed at the expectant faces, the genuine interest, as I look out from the pulpit, and pray that what I say is worth their attention, and acceptable in the sight of the Almighty. Recently, a member of the congregation said that she felt blessed that someone had read, digested and reflected on the Scriptures just for her, and each week she could come along to church knowing that she would learn something new, or hear something to make her think. As we turn to the sacrament there is a reverence and dignity as old and young approach the altar and meet their God. And just before we go on our way, we hear what the children have been doing in Sunday school, and with amazement realize that the stories of our faith can be told with shoeboxes, pipe-cleaners and toilet rolls.

As one congregation leaves another enters. Perhaps a baptism, hundreds of guests with their mobile phones, gift bags and party outfits, followed by an afternoon service for families with very young children. Both are noisy, interactive affairs and the congregations are inquisitive about this thing called 'faith', but cautious. They have worshipped, and some have, indeed, doubted. These occasions present another chance to talk about what really matters: love, hope, faith, forgiveness, peace, new life. The challenge is to offer people a way in, an apology for what the church believes, what I believe, without slipping into ecclesial jargon or saying what they expect a vicar to say. At evensong, as the church prepares to settle down for the night, there are bells, and psalms, held together with a language from the past. Every week, exactly eleven minutes into the service, one of our regulars comes in with his bags, anorak and bicycle clips and settles down in exactly the same pew, for a snooze through the canticles, the sermon and the prayers.

At the end of the day, hundreds of people may have passed through this building. It can feel more like a railway station than a church. A convergence of lives being lived under the light of Christ, under the shadow of his wings. This is no empty shell. There is no more extraordinary educational context than a parish church. There is no place where such a diversity of people gather week by week to learn of God and learn from one another.

I get home and meditate with a glass of wine, watching undemanding Sunday night television, exhausted and spent, but content. And what have I learned? In this church, priest and people are like a raft of pebbles at the bottom of a stream, constantly moved, shaped, dragged, smoothed; chinking up against one another as living water bubbles over us. This is a place where lessons are learned, sometimes the hard way. This is what life together means. This living and breathing church is a gift of God's grace. In this church, there is also something waiting to happen.

Into this already rich, formational, learning environment of sacred space and living community, there is another way that people learn of God. It's the obvious way. Over 350 years ago one of my predecessors made 'education' a central part of his ministry here. Edward Woolmer began small, instructing village children in the church porch. Then he secured a cottage. Poor local children were taught for the first time, and over the years this school grew, supported by the parson, the squire and the congregation. Today the parish is still served well by that same church school. Schools work and religious education for children are important for any priestly ministry, but today there is also a real and desperate need to create an ethos of Christian learning for people of all ages in our churches. We might call this catechesis, religious instruction, or 'disciple-making'. Can a parish church become a school *for* faith? A school *of divinity*? A place where people learn from worship and prayer, from participating in community life, but also from intentional, programmatic, theological learning? Can a church like this be that kind of place, which allows people to learn God's ways, and offers them the opportunity to do so, creatively, holistically and honestly? There is an urgency to this question, as knowledge of the Christian faith slips from the consciousness of society and the discipline of learning, of *being shaped* by its process, is replaced by the lure of instant information. Today knowledge is a commodity. Yet we give ours away for free.

The kind of knowledge we can offer here is incomplete; some would say it is worthless. It is elusive and mysterious and yet life-changing. Somehow we have to pass the knowledge on, proclaim afresh the gospel in this generation, but how do we do that? In the Ordinal, there is a clear commission for all priests to be 'teachers'. What does that now mean? What should we be teaching and how should we be teaching it?

'A school for the local Service' RS

A vocation to teach

When I reflect on the learning that has shaped me, one priest stands out. He prepared me for confirmation. Noel was exquisitely intelligent, passionate, unrelenting in his determination to communicate something of the wonder of God and the life of Jesus Christ. There were no concessions. As we sat in the vestry Noel would use poetry and song and theology and science to help us glimpse the glory of God. We were in no doubt that faith was of vital importance. It was the centre of the universe. The utter seriousness of this endeavour was made very clear: it felt as if we were being initiated into the meaning of everything. This was no game, but life or death.

It was only about twenty years later that I fully realized what an influence this had had on me. I was asked to preach at Noel's funeral, and as I reflected on what I would say it was clear that I had come to ordination in part through the ministry of a remarkable priest who had a serious vocation to teach, preach and learn. The library he left behind was extraordinary. Here was a parish priest who mined down into the depths of theology to inform his ministry. He would read and write in Greek and Hebrew, his bookshelves were heavily laden with classics and with original works of twentieth-century theology – Barth, Bonhoeffer, Tillich; there were biblical commentaries and works of philosophical theology, biographies, literary novels in English, Russian and German; poetry, drama, music and art history. I learned that in retirement Noel became a valued interlocutor of atheists, agnostics and doubters. He loved to wrangle with theology, to test it out and find new ways to express that serious matter of the gospel of Jesus Christ, which he knew could completely transform someone's life. His vocation to teach was equally balanced by his willingness to learn, and by the humility that understood that in the end all knowledge was but as straw when face to face with the Almighty. The more books there were, the more provisional his learning became. Noel was indeed a catechist, but he was also a seeker, a searcher, a pilgrim, and he never stopped being a catechumen. His apparently complete library served to remind me that to teach the faith we have to be aware that our intellectual knowledge is merely a prelude to what God reveals. It is always going to be incomplete.

So how do you teach a mystery? How do you communicate something that cannot be fully known? How do you teach people love and longing and worship? Perhaps our pedagogy should reflect this conundrum. Can we teach through worship and prayer, through dialogue, conversation and story, in a way that is not didactic, or authoritarian, not a final answer but the beginning of a question? As teachers of the faith are we happy to make mistakes, change our mind, and be corrected? Can we seek out learning in everything that we do – even in everything that we are – and let God teach us that we may see the divine in all things and at all times? When one considers the way Christ taught his disciples, such a model seems to fit. Stories, parables, riddles, questions, challenges. He let people grow their own mind. And he taught by example: 'Follow me,' he said.

Teach me, my God and King

The pure directness of George Herbert's 'Teach me, my God and King' has always made the mundane sparkle with the reality of the incarnation. It has woken me to meaning in apparently meaningless circumstances. For any action or task that I am given, it is down to me to see within it the divine, to allow God to teach me that there is nothing 'not good enough' for God to inhabit. It is perhaps the obligation and duty of any priest, in the long shadow of St Benedict, to allow herself to be schooled in wisdom and taught by God through study and prayer, to find in the seemingly pointless and functional some kind of point and purpose, making the endeavour of learning part of our way of being, part of our ontology as priests in the world today, in order that we in turn may teach of God using whatever means we might find. We perhaps shouldn't be surprised that we are called to teach not only with what we say, or what we do, or what we know, but with who we are. But we are *becoming*; we are not static or complete beings; maybe the most important thing we can do is admit that we are still learning, that we don't have all the answers.

In any parish church, worship is the first teacher. This is particularly pertinent in acts of worship when most of those attending are at the very beginning of their encounter with the faith. The occasional offices are an obvious example – when the priest welcomes and the church hosts potentially hundreds of people who may want to taste and see. I remember two occasions when worship and prayer seemed to have taken sudden root in people's lives, and God the teacher was a tangible presence.

Because our mid-afternoon family service is non-eucharistic, we were trying to explore ways in which we could introduce some kind of sacramental action into the liturgy. The services are normally quite noisy, and mostly parents and children alike are new to worship. On the feast of the Transfiguration, we tried the oldest trick in the book. We invited families to walk up to the altar with a tea-light, and light it as a prayer – pray for something in your life that needs to be changed or transformed, we said. In near complete silence, thirty families with young children approached the altar of God. The children were awestruck; their parents, many with babes in arms, came to the altar thoughtfully; something was happening. Was it the candles, the procession to the altar, the music, the invitation to participate?

On another occasion, we held a 'teaching Eucharist' for the junior school children. Each year they came over to church to look at the architecture as part of their topic on 'places of worship', but we invited them to join our regular midweek congregation and participate. The service was explained, each little thing we did was elucidated by a narrator; and although none of the children were going to receive communion, we felt it was important to celebrate the Eucharist together, so they could see how important this bread and wine was to those Christians they were learning about in class. After songs, a reading, a mini-sermon and prayers, the children were invited with their teachers to come for a blessing, if they wished, and because our church is ancient and awkward, the only way to do this was by inviting them to the communion rail.

The children watched the regular congregation come forward to receive the sacrament, and then they came too. We suggested that they come with a silent prayer in their hearts, or with something they wanted to say to God. Again and again, children would quietly come forward, kneel at the rail, bow their heads, put their hands together and pray. Just like that. In fact, some of them were so caught up in prayer, they remained for what seemed like hours, kneeling before the Lord their maker. The teachers eventually had to move them on. Just leave them, I thought. Let them stay all day long. They were hungry for prayer, hungry for God.

Then there is the more programmatic learning that church communities often engage in: Bible studies, home groups, Lent courses, and so on. One Lent, we decided we would have a 'School of Prayer', where each week we explored a different tradition of praying. We explored *lectio divina*, the Jesus Prayer, praying with icons, the Ignatian examen, silence, and the music of Taizé. For me, as a priest, this kind of activity was liberating; teaching on prayer seemed to me exactly what I should be doing. The most popular session was the session on icons. By pure fluke I discovered a well-respected Orthodox icon writer living in the parish. He mentioned that he hadn't done many talks before, and was a little nervous, but he came along, and spoke about the 'art' – the paints and brushes he used, and the symbolism, and how he was trained in a monastery on Mount Athos. What struck me, as he spoke, was his depth of knowledge. He said that an iconographer is first and foremost a theologian. He was serious about his faith. His whole life and work was a kind of pointer or prelude to the revelation of God in creation. As he spoke, timidly at first, everyone was enraptured by what he said. There was a hush. Again it felt as if we were being initiated into the meaning of life itself. His passion and his prayerfulness were infectious; I think the heart of every person in that room was aflame. People didn't want to go home.

For the last four years we have been running something called 'Friday Night Theology'. Each session explores a different contemporary question – our tag line is 'a space for questions ... but we promise no easy answers'. We wanted to create a space for people to think, to question, to ponder issues that affect life today or that pique our imagination. It was OK to get to the end of a session and not have everything neatly sewn up. We fully expected people to leave with more questions than answers, but at least the question would have been raised and curiosity would have been kindled; who knows if it would ever lead to illumination?

We have explored the pertinent, the important, the esoteric, and the plain daft. Issues that perhaps people thought the church wouldn't be interested in. Do you believe in angels? Do aliens exist? Can you be Christian and a scientist? Do pets go to heaven? Does God care about cancer? How do you train a priest? Does anyone care about the environment? Religion and politics don't mix – or do they? Who's afraid of Richard Dawkins? Do ghosts exist? We start with a pithy question, and then get down to some serious dialectic. We often invite guest speakers, who are warned that we like to leave plenty of time for questions; my role as I carry the roving microphone around the church is that of a facilitator, encouraging questions and enabling discussion. More often than not, the conversation spills out from the church and into the pub next door, exactly as we wanted it to do.

What has surprised me has been the hunger for this kind of learning, not just from within the church but from beyond it. Naming something Friday Night Theology couldn't possibly be a winner, could it? This has to be the most unattractive title ever, I thought as I stuck up posters in the library. But people came. Our usual attendance is about fifteen to twenty, but some subjects have brought in up to seventy people eager to learn more. I have heard from other colleagues that similar intentionally 'theological' discussion groups are becoming popular in many parishes – not just with the regulars either; the fringes are being drawn in. Could theology be missional? People want to debate, to discuss. It seems that we want to wrestle with God (and one another), to handle and examine Scripture and theology rather than cover these things in bubble wrap, only to be used on special occasions by specially authorized people. Are we seeing a democratization of theological learning? From my experience, it seems that people don't want someone to tell them what to think or believe, they want to embark on their own explorations, and the miraculous thing is that sometimes they come to a church to begin that learning journey. Wouldn't it be amazing if every church in the land could be a place of wonder and learning – schools for faith, with open doors and open minds and open to God? Could the humble parish church be the seedbed of a new kind of enlightenment? Academies for teaching the mystery?

While we were on a roll with Friday Night Theology, we came up with something else, equally unfashionable: an annual lecture. There *were* comments. 'Who do they think they are at St Michael's?' I heard people whisper. 'A cathedral?' But we didn't care. The murmuring spoke of that lack of both aspiration and confidence that often blights the Church. Why couldn't we have an annual parish lecture, and invite faith-based speakers to the doorstep? Looking through the parish magazines of the last century, guest speakers and preachers were the norm. Northern provincial churches like this, churches of no particular note, had no qualms about inviting speakers from Bradford, York, or even London! It seems that in the past the educative potential of the parish church was more fully understood. The lecture was really an impact occasion, a focus, a little bit of icing on the educational cake. But doing something like this gave people confidence and pride in what a church could be. Relevant, inspirational, educational. It was really possible to be a place where serious learning could happen at all sorts of levels. A place where people weren't afraid to ask difficult questions. Herbert says that in sermons and prayers, 'men may sleep or wander'. But, he adds, 'when one is asked a question, he must discover what he is'. In that sense, much of our parish learning began with a question and ended with a question; we were constantly trying to discover what we were before God.

A vocation to learn

Like my predecessors, I have felt the urgency of keeping education at the heart of my priestly identity and at the heart of parish ministry – but I have had to fight hard for it. The reality is that teaching and learning for the priest come a poor second to management and administration; and that 'seriousness' that Noel and our iconographer embodied can be dissipated very easily. I have often played my learning down and acted the fool. I have often sidelined study as being a luxury in my ministry rather than the bread and butter of it. There is sometimes little time to feed one's own mind and heart in order to feed the minds and hearts of a congregation. It's a constant struggle. And if you do find an hour or so to engage in study, you feel guilty, or lazy, and will be interrupted by multiple phone calls, the ping of emails or someone knocking at the front door. Ministry can quickly become arid without the life that comes from the water of divine wisdom. Current ecclesial policies are often shaped by outcomes and ticking boxes to demonstrate competence rather than learning for the sheer joy and wonder of getting to know God. Many diocesan formation days are about management or leadership and yet I, and I'm sure many others, yearn for input on prayer, Bible study, theology, or indeed anything more imaginative than dealing with conflict or managing multiple congregations. Please, give us poetry, song, history, science, music! – anything to expand our minds and liberate our thinking.

These days much priestly study takes place in order to write a sermon – the most obvious and the most undervalued catechetical tool we have. I love preaching, but I feel that my preparation time is squeezed, and the sermon I end up preaching is usually the first draft of a better sermon I feel I could have preached if I'd had more time to devote to it. Herbert speaks of catechizing through preaching, and how this form of catechesis is first a sermon to oneself, and then to others, so that the priest may also grow with the growth of his flock. There seems to be an acknowledgement that the spiritual growth of a priest is somehow connected to the spiritual growth of the parish.

I thought again of Noel and the iconographer. These were people for whom learning about God was at the heart of everything. The only 'outcome' from their study was adoration, but this attracted others to come closer to God. For me theological study has often felt as if it's been at the very bottom of a long list of other tasks that I must complete before the week is out. The idea of a study day, or time out to read or reflect, is for most of us pie in the sky. The second coming seems more likely. Many a time I have felt intellectually malnourished and in need of solid food.

In his introduction to *Love's Endeavour, Love's Expense*, W. H. Vanstone, one of Manchester's famous clerical sons, captures in words a sense of connection between the prayerful wisdom he received from God and the action and sense of purpose he was inspired to initiate in his ministry. Vanstone received this wisdom in a moment of what he calls 'intellectual clarity'. He says that this insight, this wisdom, spoke to him of the importance of the Church 'coming-to-be'. It was, if you will, the prelude to his ministerial action in the outer housing estates of Halliwell and Kirkholt, Lancashire, a very different context from my suburban country parish. He goes on to describe how this wisdom 'emerged in action', or, he says, 'invested action with an entirely new sense of purpose'.[1] Through his own personal devotion to study and prayer, Vanstone was swept up in potentiality, allowing his life and ministry to point towards the greater work, which was God's.

In his poetic autobiography, *The Growth of a Poet's Mind*, also called *The Prelude*, Wordsworth sets his whole life as a prelude to his literary corpus. Perhaps the priest can also inhabit this kind of position, where in Christ there is always more to see, and more to find; the Christian life, and by God's grace, the priestly life, being a foretaste of what is to come, to all that will one day be fulfilled. In this light, the knowledge of the priest is always destined to be formative and transformative, yet incomplete – because we know only in part, we are all a work in progress, yearning to know and to be fully known.

The gospel of Jesus Christ can truly turn the lives of those who follow upside down. I have seen it myself. It's a real privilege to see people grow in faith and discipleship before your eyes, to see people take those tentative first steps, or experience those seismic shifts with which God often surprises us. Walking with people to baptism, or confirmation, or indeed ordination, is surely why we get ordained in the first place. To see lives changed by faith, to see people learning of God in Christ and coming to know him more fully is wondrous, and to be involved in a tiny part of that process is more than any of us deserve. It's a delight and a blessing to see people hungry to know more about God; and this miracle happens more often than we could ever imagine possible given our narrative of ecclesial decline. People do have a desire to learn of divine things – and the role of the priest and the role of the Church is to point them towards that divinity. This is where the priest in teaching, and the parish in its mission, is called to always be pointing to something greater. 'The Catechism is towards Divinity,' Herbert says.

---

1 W. H. Vanstone, *Love's Endeavour, Love's Expense* (London: DLT, 1977), p. 16.

It seems to me that this desire for God, this hunger to know God, should be at the very heart of parish ministry and the priestly vocation. The role of the priest and the parish is to deal in possibilities and potential, creativity and renewal. If the Church is a kind of school without knowing it, then priests are teachers, translators, interpreters, communicators, apologists and catechists – and at the same time catechumens. We are just a prelude to what God the teacher can do. If we embrace that vocation, if we are prepared to share it generously, something might indeed happen. Something might change.

Office: Funerals

JESSICA MARTIN

South Cambridgeshire

This is a chapter on the nature of memory and remembering, and of leaning upon God's changelessness in the way we live, and the way we celebrate, our mortality.

The villages I serve are built on chalk. The precise, mechanically dug sides of a grave are sometimes almost white: straight, pale beige walls with paler friable lumps in them. Few roots. Between the powdery dryness of the medium and the faint chemical reek of the coffin, it is hard to imagine that the body lowered in will turn again to its earth.

I turn towards the stiff faces of the mourners and tell them, raising my voice to compensate for the deadening effects of the open air, that we are seasonal ephemera. 'Our days are like the grass,' I say. 'When the wind blows over it, it is gone, and its place shall know it no more.' The headstone will go up at the end of the six-month settling period, when the mound of chalky earth finally falls as coffin and body disintegrate together. Often – embalming seems a pretty thorough process – it takes longer.

I tell them that the merciful goodness of the Lord endures when human beings don't. The mourners are preoccupied with getting through it and the words wash past them: God-talk. But the older I get, and the more funerals I take, the more that sentence comforts me. 'Thy lovingkindness is better than life,'

we say to God as part of the diurnal rhythm of the psalms.
That's a thought experiment worth venturing towards. What
does it mean? Is it really our salvation that God endures? Is the
name of that salvation lovingkindness?

The people who choose burial are, on the whole, the ones for
whom place matters, the ones who believe that the place will go
on knowing them when people no longer can. The last village
burial I took reunited two shy brothers who had lived together
all their adult lives; the next grave along is their longstanding
next-door neighbour. At the wake, older villagers told stories
of the dead man as a child, stuck in a wheelchair with TB ('He
wasn't allowed to set foot on the floor for a year!') and how
he persuaded them to push him down the hill and then let go
at an angle, so that the wheelchair careered into the pub wall.
There's still the pub. When I buried the ashes of a man who
had sold insurance locally house to house a mourner stood
reading the slate tablets for a while after the service, looking
over the 'designated ashes area'. He said to the new grave,
'Well, Roy, I think you know everybody here?' Up at the village cemetery, where the full burials happen, the parish clerk
will negotiate, delicately, about who goes in which grave plot.
'I couldn't possibly put those two together; they, you know,
they had their differences, over the years. But *these* two, well,
they were always such good neighbours, they will be company
for each other.'

At the crematorium, it's different. People expect – not to forget, necessarily, but to be forgotten. The structure of the place
forces it upon them. It's a location for all names and none. It's
set up for remembrance, of course, in lots of ways; every square
inch of the attractive municipal garden area is filled with commemorative memorabilia (you hire your spot for twenty-five
years only); the stones of the courtyard where they put the
flowers bristle with names and dates (but are no longer available); often the flowers themselves speak: 'Nan', 'Granddad',
'Mum', written in bright white petals caged with wire. But the

sheer bulk, the throughput, the time pressure – the words fade and vanish with the flowers and leave behind metal or plastic skeletons. There are no local ties, no adjacent neighbours. No shared history. It's not a place for the living to abide. Whatever you think of the standard funeral reading from John 14.1–6 about the many dwelling places of 'my Father's house', everyone knows that none are to be found here. The car park is full of departing people briskly snapping their cars open with electronic keys, loud with relief. They will do their long grieving somewhere else.

One man for whose family I took a crematorium funeral (his third bereavement in eighteen months) decided, without consultation, that black humour was the way to cope, so as the curtains closed on his mother's coffin the *Countdown* music played its jaunty 'time's up!' twiddle. Nothing could have said more eloquently that he knew she would be forgotten. It was the same mixture of gallantry and despair on the edge of futile nothing that chooses, at fully post-Christian funerals, to play 'Always Look On The Bright Side', with its visual imprint of multiple crucified bodies and the punchline: 'Life's a piece of shit/ When you look at it.' That's how the English celebrate loss. The *Countdown* effect was kinder and funnier – and a lot less plaintive than the other national favourite, 'Don't Stop Me Now', with the soaring dead voice of Freddie Mercury still repeating and repeating, from his place in the recorded frieze of hedonist saints: 'I'm having a good time! I'm having a ball! Don't stop me now! ... I don't want to stop at all!'

I am not, of course, asked to take 'secular' funerals. And mostly the dead for whom I officiate have not been having a good time but a weary slog through slow bodily closedown. The families who ask the vicar to take the funeral are honouring someone's faith, though it is not always clear whose; faith is a buffer against meaninglessness and it's not necessary to ask who among the dead and the mourners possesses the gift. The vicar will do faith for them. For their part they'll attempt to avert mortal despair by telling life stories: The

Eulogy; Memories of ... Doris, Maisie, Kathleen, Frank, Roy. Fury against mortality is usually kept at bay in such rituals (and often the hard work of dying has altered, even dissipated, its force) – but it hovers, and life stories can't always send it away. One older widow, exhausted with the effort of caring for a man wholly unwilling even to consider his own extinction, quietly subverts the children's weeping efforts to reconstruct their father in the easy generous image of his younger self by reading Dylan Thomas in a voice of flat conviction: 'Rage, rage against the dying of the light.'

But this is unusual. More often it is the generic poem that exhorts mourners to 'move on': 'You can close your eyes and mourn that she/he has died, or you can open your eyes and be glad that she/he has lived ... Live, love, and go on.' It's highly adaptable. You just switch pronoun according to the gender of the deceased. Or it's Henry Scott Holland announcing the dead are only in the next room. Or the writer of the pantheistic poem that finds the dead person dissipated into the beauty of the physical world: 'I am the thousand winds that blow.' I don't mind that so much. It's not exactly Christian but at least it's not, emotionally, nonsense. No one in my experience has ever chosen to express the self-withholding mortal rebelliousness of the traditional funeral psalm, Psalm 39: 'I held my tongue, and spake nothing: I kept silence, even from good words, but it was pain and grief to me ... tell me the number of my days ... O spare me a little, before I go hence and am no more seen.' Only once have I ever uttered that: at the funeral in a posh church in London, of a friend robbed of speech by a brain tumour. He had asked for the traditional service for the Burial of the Dead in the 1662 *Book of Common Prayer*. Most of the congregation assumed the psalm to have been chosen especially for his situation. They were nearly right.

The *Countdown* couple have found their church connection a help with the three bleak deaths – two mothers and a father – they have had to deal with in a short space of time. It helps not because they are believers but because they are toiling at the vanishing work of memory, and village churches and churchyards are material versions of memory palaces.[1] All three parents died with dementia and had at least partly forgotten who they were. Witnessing their fragmentation was worse than anything in their physical extinction. 'We haven't the gift of faith,' explains the son with touching formality, as we try to find an acceptable biblical passage before the third and last of the funerals. It's taken all three occasions – with their visits, conversations and wakes – to find the trust to say this.

Yet the same year he and his wife stage a concert, in the church, of the bluegrass gospel music they love, dividing the proceeds between church funds and the Alzheimer's Society. As they play you can see them relax into the borrowed idiom of the faith they don't profess. We sing 'May The Circle Be Unbroken', and it becomes possible to weep as well as joke. Afterwards we have a jam at the pub with some local folk musicians and I'm happy: it's been so long since I've been part of that quick, responsive dance of pattern and opportunity that you get when you're improvising with other players, seeing the moment, or seeing someone else's moment come and standing back for it, watching the weave of the shape in the air between us growing in the miniature sphere of time we have, three or four minutes of conversing voices: there, made and gone.

The following year a card naming the dead of that family appears in the church porch by the door: 'Never forgotten'. There's a niche in the local memory palace for a few more names. At All Souls, 2 November, that month for remembering the dead, we will speak the names of more and more people, fill up the pews with more and more of the bereaved. The service grows every year.

Unlike 'real' memory palaces, churches are physically rather than imaginatively mnemonic; every material reminder has weight and heft. And they aren't all cards. The load of a church's

---

1 A memory palace is a mental construction to aid the work of recollection: you imagine an architectural space and put the fact or object to be remembered in one of its rooms or niches.

past can seem to leave little room for the living, because its monumental backlog – overt and covert, plaques and pews and hassocks, brasses and candles, flower vases and carpets – is so vast. This is, sometimes, the church being treated as if it were its own point; the building as eternity itself, God's only home. After a very few years there is a lot to remember; historically, those who have had the largest and longest memorials have been those able to pay for them. So the church's relationship to memory is materially tricky to negotiate as well. For every headstone, legible or illegible, there are many forgotten bodies buried in wool.

Churches are signs of change and decay at least as insistently as they are emblems of remembrance. That is what causes all the panic about their fabric, rather as the signs of our own age-ing bodies create mortal fear. Some parishioners struggle for the courage to walk through the churchyard to the (popular, delicious, award-winning, local) coffee morning, they are so terrified of the graves; others associate the interior of the church entirely with the grisly business of their beloved's funeral and just can't walk in through the door any more. Church = death. But many more contrive to creep in, alone, to sit below the light falling from the windows and recollect their beloved dust in silence. These are the ones who will battle for nothing at all to be changed in the church furniture, will give generously to mend the roof, preserve a transept or tower or carving, join the church cleaning rota. They will very seldom come to a service to swell the 'average Sunday attendance' (ASA) figures. ASA is now a decisive measure for many diocesan discussions as to whether there should be a local memory palace at all. Many will stop being churches soon, will no longer point towards eternity or community; the only sign they will offer to this generation will be a sign of the times. They will become quirky real estate opportunities for monied buyers looking for something a bit different – breakfast bars in the chancel, mezzanine bedroom platforms in the transepts, flatscreen TV in the clerestories, wetroom where the font once stood. They will become private property, with sophisticated alarm systems, and no one will / creep in to see the light fall there any more.

On the top of the churchyard wall, weathered and almost unrecognizable, are carved shapes of swift-moving animals: a horse, perhaps a deer, a slim-waisted dog. Forty years ago an autocratic churchwarden made a decision not to attempt to preserve them and now they are nearly invisible. The brightest signs of eternity point towards God through vanishing moments; shift with light, years and weather; disappear sooner or later out of human vision and into the gaze of the light perpetual towards which they are running. The human gifts we can no longer see or feel sanctify the sacred places where we learn to pray and learn to die: the earth full of our ancestors' bones, the vanished artefacts, the histories that disappeared when the minds' repositories broke and spilled, blossoming in the dust. Perhaps the churches, as they fall into ruin, will blossom too.

Modern imperatives to remember and record have become widespread, even near-universal – the capturing of life-events via different media now a cultural imperative almost stronger than actually living our lives. The 'spontaneous' public face is a difficult art to learn, with complex rules. Its spreading power has a big impact on funerals. It has become transgressive not to have a eulogy, ordinary to have photographs both on the service order and afterwards at the reception – sometimes along with video footage. In line with the increasing reluctance to use the word 'funeral' (the favoured title on service sheets is 'A Celebration of the Life of ...'), upbeat narratives are expected and indeed are central. Their ideal function: to gather up a neat-ish summary version of the person who has died, which people will enjoy recognizing but which will also contain some not too disruptive surprises.

The overt intention of a eulogy is to preserve a person's essence. This is admirable, understandable and problematic. As I listen to eulogies – or give them – I notice what they cannot disclose or record. They have, perhaps mercifully, little to do with the perspective and particular memories stilled in the brain of the corpse in the fake wood box. The bulk of those lost memories would seem irrelevant at best to the collector of neat narrative data, and some would disrupt it troublingly – the unacknowledged affair, the rebellious thought or act about one's children, the unwished flowerings of different kinds of desire, the flailings of disinhibited old age. One function of funeral life-narrative is to overlay and suppress the stuff that doesn't fit, perhaps especially the utterances of anger, bewilderment, pain or mischief that issue from dying minds and bodies. And, indeed, why should these private sufferings be obtruded into public space? I don't think they should. There is sometimes a moment in the funeral planning when they can be talked about (almost furtively) by relatives haunted by death's ugly pains and indignities, or by the grim medical decisions that belong to slower extinctions. But the speed with which eulogy consigns it all to forgetfulness is troubling too. There seems to be little room to acknowledge suffering. Expressions of disruptive anguish tend to be classified as nonsense in the hope that they can then be disregarded; should *Why hast thou forsaken me?* always be edited out of the story?

Eulogy reinstates a vanished health and stability, reconstructs a person on the lines needed by the mourners. It is a difficult form to manipulate, requiring a skill and tact beyond most speakers to do well and running athwart usual modern understandings of 'sincere' which favour disruptive disclosure – the very last thing wanted in this particular context. At times the wish to provide competing versions of the dead person will cause tension between relatives. What is considered primary and what secondary, or even unimportant, can be a matter for pain. For some, the whole narrative enterprise can be a kind of compulsory last straw.

So: I sit at a table with four polite, middle-class people who seem unusually constrained, with me, and with each other. I can see something's going on, but not what. They don't meet my eyes.

'I suppose it's usual to have a eulogy?' one of them says.

'People often do, but you don't have to.'

'I think we should. You'll do it, I hope?'

'Yes, of course. Would you like to tell me something about him? What would you like to have remembered?'

A long, unhappy pause.

Someone ventures, 'He liked shopping at Asda.'

More silence. Someone else has a go. 'He was the slowest cyclist I've ever seen.'

And no one else can say anything at all.

Or: another woman, widow to a locally born petty criminal who has died of drink in his sixties, says to me that she'd like me to put together a eulogy for him. She's sure she wants one. But I ask her what she'd like me to say, and she just looks at me. What should she tell me to put into his life story? Do I talk about him joking and flirting with the nurses during his final hospitalization for liver failure? The estrangement of half his family, including some of his children? Being laid off from the forklifts for being constantly pissed? We gaze at each other across the filthy, bare room, enlivened only by a wall clock of monotonously copulating cartoon rabbits, mutually helpless. Eventually, at the funeral itself, the widow is released into tears as the exit music plays 'You Were Always On My Mind', a song about a man who loved better than he behaved.

The terminally ill man with whom I prayed on a Friday evening for four years refused to have a funeral. He gave his brain to medical science (his body, to his irritation, was too damaged to be useful); we celebrated communion in his sitting room, bathed in the cold sunlight of early spring; said goodbye over a beer (his) in the hospice. He was grieved, but entirely serene. He asked for a choral evensong, and nothing said about his life, and that's what he got; but it was a visible strain, social and personal, for those who loved him to have no farewell ritual, no ordered account of his impact upon the world he had left.

But the trumpets sounded on the other side for our own Mr Great-Heart, just the same.

Funeral services are designed to assist the transition between the companionship of being and the lonelier work of recollection. Eulogies have, of course, a clear role here; so do the carefully chosen photographs, the recorded music. With all their problems, these are good functional signposts. The liturgy is much more ambiguously placed, struggling with a complex theological history as well as the enormous range of pastoral situations it is supposed to address.

It's 1,600 years since Augustine warned a friend not to trust visions of the dead in paradise, and 500 (more or less) since the Reformers blew up the bridge between the dead and the living, forbidding priests to address the dead directly, offer prayers for their welfare, or opine anything at all about their ultimate destination. *Common Worship* follows suit; the only prayers that allow the officiant to address the dead are in the section marked 'Prayers with the dying' – assuming a largely fictional situation in which priests will be sitting at the deathbeds of parishioners as a matter of course. (It happens, of course, but to be there within even an hour of someone's death is rare, and usually it is the hour that follows, not the hour that precedes the last breath.) One is not supposed to say, 'Go, Christian soul' when the soul has already left the body; but in the first space for ceremonial order since the mess and rush of the CPR, the tangle of tubes, the fatal, choking discovery that you can no longer swallow, or whatever it is; will our eternal God mind if the living send the dead on their way with a farewell there was no time for in the chaotic battle of dying? I don't think so.

The Reformers had their reasons; but the heart has its reasons, too, and most people just ignore this 'don't talk to the dead' stuff. The churchyards and cemeteries are full of people chatting to their buried relatives, reading them stories, leaving birthday cards and teddy bears (wrapped in cellophane against the wet) on graves. The benefice prayer list makes a distinction between 'X and family' (living) and 'the family of X' (where X is dead, and therefore can notionally no longer be prayed for, so the bereaved are prayed for instead). It's often ignored. I'd

take bets that few understand it. The licensed lay ministers, low
church though they are, pray for the dead unselfconsciously;
they understand instinctively the need for the living to hear
words of care and attention called across the broken bridge.
Just as when people are dying their relatives want to hear them
named in church, so when they have died their spoken names
seem to keep them within the unbroken circle for just a little
longer. I find I can't quite pray for the dead (what I am praying
for for the dead?); I fall back on the oldest prayers and invoke
upon them perpetual light, eternal rest – still wondering what I
mean, caught up in the mystery of the phrase.

So: the *Common Worship* funeral service is talkative about
Christian hope, vague on the universal nature of its applic-
ability, grudgingly tolerant of eulogy, unrealistically insistent
on congregational penitence, and just as uncompromising as its
sixteenth-century predecessor, *The Book of Common Prayer*,
about the inadmissibility of treating the dead as part of the
same community as the living.

Admittedly the liturgy has a lot to cope with. Nominally the
rite of an Established Church, a tiny proportion of those for
whom it is used will be religiously observant; yet the generous
Hookerian rule that you treat all as saved and leave judgement
to God shoves the text so firmly towards universalism that it
feels it must shove back by banging on a lot about personal
faith. I'm not sure this works very well. Better by far to stick to
the grounds for faith than to court danger by making hopeful
confessional remarks, via the officiant, which assume mourners
to be making indirect testimony to the dead man or woman's
faith and practice. It's unfair as well as unrealistic to foist such
declarations, even indirectly, on that congregation, though I
imagine the intention is to be inclusively collaborative in theological mood rather than authoritarian.

Common Worship in other ways takes absolutely the point
that pastorally funerals are for the living rather than the dead
and this is its main governing principle; but the generous room
the BCP makes for mortal bitterness *Common Worship* feels it

cannot afford; so instead it has some rather mawkish prayer options about shock, trauma, refusal and the healing of memories. It also frontloads a penitence few will find emotionally intelligible from a standing start. If you've already decided to suppress a mass of difficulties in the eulogy you aren't all that likely to want to ask God's forgiveness during the service. ('We don't want anything too gloomy; this is a celebration.') So while penitence may in fact make perfect emotional sense, it is so alien to public cultural discourse that people will neither want it nor be able to use it if it is foisted on them. The 'Kyrie' space is the closest one can ever get.

I do not always feel that the dead – and I have now buried a significant proportion of those who welcomed me in 2010 – are very far away, or that death itself is a very distant prospect in general. Sometimes its ambience seems catching: permeating clothes and skin, mind and breath. During the winter, when the old begin to die and the young and middle-aged submit to the greed of their cancers, I feel as if I carry illness and death along with me daily, a version of my own exhaustion. At these times the young W. H. Auden's words echo mockingly in my head: 'That spot on your skin is the shocking disease'. Easy for him to laugh. He was young then. Sometimes the spot on your skin *is* a shocking disease.

Funerals carry an enormous emotional charge. They are genuinely transitional. Following funerals I feel almost ill with the weight of others' grief: haunted, or poisoned. After one funeral for a child, I heard the Taylor Swift song with which her big sisters accompanied the collage of pictures of her life over and over, sleeplessly for two nights. Then, mercifully, one evening in the garden in the dark, the sick feeling disappeared and with it the repeating music. I have never, thank God, been able to recall it. I wonder if I would even recognize it if I heard it?

You live well, say the writers of seventeenth-century devotions, when you live in the light of eternity. *Common Worship* retains a prayer section with that name, containing some ancient prayers, lightly modernized, which speak of God's purposes for those who die. This, it seems to me, is an acknowledgement that death does not mark the end of the work God makes of our fleeting lives, either in the world or out of it, and I am comforted. In spite of the Reformers, we are not without a bridge. Our fleetingness and God's endlessness meet together in the divine humanity of Jesus, and he reconciles the one with the other. That is what I think redemption is. With that in mind, maybe learning to live in the light of eternity is actually to come to terms with being a creature who dies, and is lost, and yet by gift is for ever held in the eye of God's continual now. I hope so.

One day, feeling particularly low about the death of a fine and much-loved parishioner, I took myself off to the cemetery to visit his grave. It's full of rabbits, this cemetery; everyone complains at the way they eat all the flowers. ('We've sent the ferrets down again, but it hasn't made that much difference, I am afraid.') The only thing the rabbits won't touch is hellebore. It was a raw day, the grave space denuded as usual. Ralph was under the earth. I stood there for a long time, looking out over the fields, getting chilly, with nothing to say and nothing to know, wondering what on earth I thought I was doing in the cure of souls, and getting no answer.

Overhead, a harsh sound, like the air tearing: a great flock of wild geese, flying high. And I know they were just geese, but they carried paradise visions: messages from the far country.

PART 3

Faith, Hope and Love

In Praise of Flaking Walls

To be alive is to throw shadows.
No mere ghost could obstruct the light
like we do. This much we know:

that to be made incarnate
is to be as solid as the limewashed wall,
to come from rumour, hope, to weight.

We know that sheets of stucco crumble
under frost and sun, that every flaw
is nailed by lichen, that all

this is provisional. We know more:
that such beautiful distress – a stone
wall turned to mud and straw –

will be mirrored in our own,
that mountains will give way to snow,
that light will look through us again.

Michael Symmons-Roberts

The Priest Attends to the Signs of the Times: Anxious Toil and Daily Bread

ALEX HUGHES

Southsea, Portsmouth

This summary of the faithful marginality of the priest affirms that all we need is in God's good provision. He affirms the primary duty of prayer and study as a rich soil for all ministry, and points towards a wider eschatological horizon than 'calculated viability'.

A few days before I was due to be ordained my parish priest presented me with a charming antique devotional book. He hadn't been a significant figure in my journey towards ordination, which mainly happened while I was away at university, but it was a thoughtful gesture. As I thanked him for his kindness, however, he made a slightly ominous comment: 'I'm very pleased you're doing this, though I'm glad it's not me starting out now. Things have changed so much since I was ordained.' Fired with youthful enthusiasm I put this remark down to pre-retirement fatigue rather than serious disillusionment, but in the fourteen years that have elapsed since then it would be fair to say that the shine has worn off my image of ministry too.

I'm sure this is quite healthy if it means my idea of priesthood is less romantic now – after all, the best priests are often those who tend to forget (though not neglect) their priesthood. In any case my purpose is not to whinge, because although I do think some aspects of ministry have changed for the worse I don't believe there has ever been a golden age, or that there ever will be. Clergy these days are not necessarily more put upon than their dedicated predecessors and in this respect I tend to agree with John Pridmore that 'conscientious clergy are burdened more by the contradictions of their work than by its volume'.[1] In my experience, this sense of contradiction can lead to an anxious uncertainty about the priest's role, which is what I want to think about now.

I knew when I arrived in my parish in inner-city Portsmouth that I would face some major challenges, and I soon began to question how an Anglican presence could continue in the long term, except in an attenuated form. Like many clergy today I wondered anxiously about what shape ministry should take in the face of numerical decline, inappropriate buildings, financial hardship, dysfunctional relationships, lack of vision, a general disconnect between the church and the parish community, and high levels of deprivation. In such situations there is considerable pressure – both internal and external – to generate growth and overcome practical problems, which gives rise to a strong impulse to manage and strategize to the point where ministry, mission and relationships are seen in functional or instrumental terms. I know that I have struggled to resist becoming the parish manager and strategic leader, even though I believe this has a negative effect on my motivation, self-understanding and work as a priest. My sharpest insight into the way things were heading for me was when our (volunteer) parish administrator suggested that if the curate did all the midweek services it would leave me to get on with 'more important things'. At the time I was coming under fire in the local media for my church council's decision to close down some of our facilities as part of an attempt to rationalize our buildings. Some years earlier I had had some training in 'asset management', which

---

1 John Pridmore, *The Inner-City of God* (London: Canterbury Press, 2008), p. 56.

made me vow never to get involved in a major building project, but circumstances dictated otherwise.

The 'buildings issue' is one that burdens a lot of clergy today. Of course it's true that many of our finest church buildings were the fruit of episcopal, abbatial or clerical enterprise and energy. But these were works of religious devotion; and even if devotion often got tangled with ambition, the sheer scale of the ambition was surely a mark of faith, which seems a far cry from the contemporary church's drive to secure sustainability through economy and diversification. Certainly good stewardship includes trying to make the sums add up, and not pouring resources into toxic assets, but it does sometimes seem that where once our forebears competed with one another to throw vaults ever higher into the heavens, we have become very mundane, 'screwing down the furniture' (as you might in inner-city Portsmouth for fear of the bailiffs). I wonder if we are more preoccupied these days with the scarcity of resources than with the abundance of grace.[2]

Buildings are only one factor conspiring to shift attitudes, of course, as multiple elements of church life (in its current institutional form) look precarious – the age profile of congregations; the number of stipendiary ministers; finances, and so on. On the surface no one seems to panic, but we are a very anxious church, I think, and the undercurrent of anxiety has seeped into the way we operate. An obvious example is the introduction of management systems.

I am not against management *per se*, and it is very frustrating to find oneself on the receiving end of *bad* management. What concerns me is that management is not ideologically neutral, so we should not welcome it uncritically.[3] Management becomes especially attractive when things are chaotic ('crisis management'), or when things are scarce ('resource management').

---

2 Sam Wells writes compellingly about scarcity and abundance in *God's Companions* (Oxford: Blackwell, 2006), ch. 1.

3 In what follows I am indebted to Philip D. Kenneson and James L. Street, *Selling Out the Church* (Nashville, TN: Abingdon Press, 1997).

It is a means of control, and it places human initiative at the centre of any enterprise. In a church context this surely invites theological interrogation. Could it be that an anxious scrabble for control is a denial of some important theological realities facing the Church today? After all, the Scriptures testify to the utmost importance of *krisis* ('judgement') and the wilderness experience. And of what scarcity could the Church complain when it still has oil and water, bread and wine? It is with regard to such far-reaching issues that I worry about ministry morphing into management – a role with no soul, perhaps. Not everyone would agree, however:

> The average pastor has been trained in religious matters. Yet, upon assuming church leadership, he is asked to run a business! Granted, that business is a not-for-profit organization, but it is still a business. The church is in the business of ministry ... Many people judge the pastor not on his ability to preach, teach, or counsel, but on his capacity to make the church run smoothly and efficiently ... In fact, even the pastor's ability to use his training in religious matters hinges on his business capabilities. He must be a good enough businessman to keep the church solvent and make it appealing enough for people to attend before he has the chance to impact upon their lives.[4]

The author of this quotation, George Barna, is a highly esteemed leader among 'church growth strategists', and while I may deplore his outlook, I suspect he discerns well the spirit of the age. If what people want are tangible results, Barna promises them by the application of carefully designed church-marketing techniques. He is fluent in the language of 'measurable outcomes' and the like – a language that has become the *lingua franca* of the modern world, from industry and business to healthcare and education. The origins of this near-universal emphasis on utility are complex, but it is typical

---

4 George Barna, *Marketing the Church* (Colorado Springs, CO: NavPress, 1988), p. 14.

of bureaucratic managerialism. As a culture it is profoundly uncongenial to religious ministry:

> What the priest is expert in – the knowledge of God – is simply no longer regarded, in practice, as very important in our society. It is not practical knowledge; it will not stand up to the pragmatic tests of the age; it accomplishes nothing.[5]

This, I think, is the root of the sense of contradiction many clergy experience, which makes us anxiously uncertain about our identity and role. Some of the most central and characteristic aspects of church life, for which ordained ministers have special responsibility, are deeply utility-resistant and cannot be brought under a scheme of 'measurable outcomes'. I think of prayer, worship and theological study in particular. Even if Barna's ideal pastor might not put such things at the top of the list of priorities, most clergy I know certainly would. Yet how often do they, like me, allow more 'productive' activities to intrude upon the time allotted for prayer and praise, with their distinctly *immeasurable* outcomes? I know only too well how easy it is to slip into thinking that no one will notice if my prayer life is thin, whereas people will berate me if I don't respond to their emails quickly enough. This is part of the reality of life today. But should it be resisted? I have always taken much comfort in some words of Monica Furlong addressed to clergy of the Diocese of Wakefield:

> I cannot speak for other laymen, but I am clear what I want from the clergy. I want them to be people who can by their own happiness and contentment challenge my ideas about status, about success, about money, and so teach me how to live more independently of such drugs. I want them to be people who can dare, as I do not dare, and as few of my contemporaries dare, to refuse to work flat out (since work is

---

5 Bryan R. Wilson, 'God in Retirement', *The Twentieth Century*, vol. 170, no. 1011 (Autumn 1961), p. 24.

an even more subtle drug than status), to refuse to compete with me in strenuousness. I want them to be people who are secure enough in the value of what they are doing to have time to read, to sit and think, and who can face the emptiness and possible depression which often attack people when they do not keep the surface of their mind occupied. I want them to be people who have faced this kind of loneliness and discovered how fruitful it is, as I want them to be people who have faced the problems of prayer. I want them to be people who can sit still without feeling guilty, and from whom I can learn some kind of tranquillity in a society which has almost lost the art. I want other things too, which you can probably imagine for yourselves, but what I want most to stress now is that what I think is very dangerous is when the clergyman becomes so desperate that he is driven to trying to beat the layman at his own game. Whereas the layman longs so much to be shown how to break out of the iron grip of a society which cuts people off from one another, makes love difficult to practise, and which tries to tell him that his spiritual life is something unimportant.[6]

This vision inspires and motivates me in my ministry because it touches something of the essence of what I believe the Church's mission is all about, in service to God's kingdom. Mission is rooted in the overflowing love of God for creation, so its practice must be governed more by lovingkindness than triumphalism, but it also necessarily involves a clash and conflict – a *krisis* in which the judgement of God is made known in human lives and in a society that will not submit to his Lordship (starting with Christians and the Church). Ken Leech is surely right, therefore, to see ministry as 'a resource against the culture, a witness against the world … organized apart from God and from spiritual values'.[7] When the pressure to *make*

---

6 Monica Furlong, 'The Parson's Role Today', a paper given at the Wakefield Diocesan Clergy Conference, April 1966.

7 Kenneth Leech, *Soul Friend* (London: DLT, 1994), p. 188.

things happen tempts the priest to wonder, 'Why ... do I kneel still/ striking my prayers on a stone/ heart?' then perhaps the commitment to prayer becomes a form of protest, its apparent uselessness exposing the vaunted efficiency that instrumentalizes every relation.[8] There is no tactic or leverage to deploy in our relationship with God, though it takes an awful lot of prayerful trying really to know this. I take it for granted, therefore, that the reason we set some people aside within the Church, and provide a stipend to relieve them of the need to be 'productive', is so that they may travel often to another place – the 'cloud of unknowing'; the 'strange new world' of the Bible – and return 'laden with pollen', that our world here may be transformed by God's elsewhere.[9] Certainly we do not want priests who are so heavenly minded as to be of no earthly use, but equally we do not want priests whose habits and ideas have been formed only by the dominant culture.

Walter Brueggemann proposes a useful analogue to reveal what is needed in this respect. Like the psychotherapist, the preacher/pastor helps God's people to abandon the script they have so far taken for granted and to enter a different script that tells the story of their life differently.[10] As I say, therefore, the vocation of the priest is to give sufficient time and attention to God's reality really to appreciate how *strange* it is, so to throw our expectations off balance and open up the possibility of a new perspective. The Scriptures, saints and artists of the Church show us again and again how reluctant we are to do this, and the subtle variety of our stratagems to avoid it.[11] We are mesmerized by the deceit of the self-evident. But the

8 R. S. Thomas, 'The Empty Church'.

9 *The Cloud of Unknowing*; Karl Barth, *The Word of God and the Word of Man*, tr. Douglas Horton (London: Hodder & Stoughton, 1935), ch. 2; R. S. Thomas, 'Somewhere'.

10 Walter Brueggemann, *The Word Militant* (Minneapolis, MN: Fortress Press, 2007), p. 32.

11 Rowan Williams has a lot to say about this in *Christ on Trial* (London: DLT, 2000), pp. 138–9 and *passim*.

summons is clear: 'Set your minds on things that are above, not on things that are on earth.'[12]

What all this means is that I am cautiously receptive to the provocations of my favourite blogger, Kim Fabricius:

> How should the church respond to congregational decline, financial deficits, and vocational shrinkage? The answer is obvious: make ministerial selection more stringent, theological education more demanding, and spiritual formation more exacting. And burn anyone who proposes a managerial or entrepreneurial solution.[13]

Like his theological hero Karl Barth, and the anti-Pelagian bent of every good theology, Fabricius invites us to be highly suspicious of humanly manufactured outcomes for the Church, which are always tainted with *hubris*. No one has put this more sharply than Dietrich Bonhoeffer: 'The figure of the Crucified invalidates all thought which takes success for its standard ... In the cross of Christ God confronts the successful man with the sanctification of pain, sorrow, humility, failure, poverty, loneliness, and despair.'[14] Of course this is counter-intuitive and scary, which is why Fabricius is concerned about the selection and training of ministers. Those who offer themselves for ordained ministry are taking a big risk, and need to be nurtured into a robust faith; for it is difficult to maintain a lifetime's confidence in prayer and theology and worship, which, like the cross, may seem foolish to the wise and weak to the powerful.[15] And it's important to stress that the responsibility here is laid upon the *whole* Church, not just the clergy.

It is sometimes said that people get the leaders they deserve, which is doubtless also often true of the Church and the

---

12 Col. 3.2.

13 Kim Fabricius, 'Doo-Doodlings', 12 December 2012 <www.faith-theology. com/2012/12/doo-doodlings.html> (accessed 17 December 2012).

14 Dietrich Bonhoeffer, *Ethics*, tr. Neville Horton Smith (London: SCM Press, 1955), p. 15.

15 1 Cor. 1.18–31.

ministry. If there is a crisis of ministry, then it is an ecclesial problem: 'When the church lacks confidence in what it is, clergy have no idea what they should be doing.'[16] When there may be almost nothing to distinguish a Christian from any other person of goodwill, apart from how they spend one hour on a Sunday morning; and when those who do come to church come to have their needs met, rather than to have their needs changed; and when the institutional angst is not about any of this, but about how to maintain the buildings and prop up the parish system, it can leave ministers wondering what they are for. As we scurry about trying to *make things happen* it can be very hard to believe and trust that *faithfulness* is all God asks of us, and that *fruitfulness* is the work of the Holy Spirit. 'For us there is only the trying. The rest is not our business.'[17]

Most clergy know only too well 'the agony/ of knowing I have little,/ and the slow job of resisting/ any attempt to make it more'.[18] It is very easy to slip into the habit of thinking that we – in our attempts to *make things happen*, to *make a difference* – are the answer to people's prayers, when of course the answer is God alone. Which is why prayer, worship and theology are crucial for ministry, as they serve to displace the self. (I realize that in saying this there is a danger of implying that they are in this respect utilitarian – that we may enter into them rightly and truly with this specific outcome in view. That would be a mistake, however, because it comes up against the fundamental problem with a utilitarian approach to value, which is that the most highly prized values of all, such as love and happiness, necessarily elude any attempt to grasp at them, and if they are pursued for their utility 'they vanish into nothing'.[19]) Frankly, I would feel too ashamed to say much about a priestly prayer life, except that it never seems to get any easier

---

16 Stanley Hauerwas and W. Willimon, 'Ministry as More Than a Helping Profession', *The Christian Century* (15 March 1989), pp. 282–4 (282).

17 T. S. Eliot, 'East Coker' (1940).

18 David Scott, 'A Priest at the Door'.

19 Iain McGilchrist, *The Master and his Emissary* (New Haven, CT: Yale University Press, 2009), p. 161.

– though this shouldn't bother us so long as we understand that prayer isn't about *making progress*. Worship, too, dies as soon as it aims at a desired effect: it is *for God*, and we have to resist the temptation to make it entertaining, and the idolatrous illusion that God can be made 'accessible' if only we order worship to cultural expectations. The place of theology at the foundation of ordained ministry perhaps deserves a bit more attention.

During the ordination service the bishop asks each ordinand to promise to be 'diligent ... in all studies that will deepen your faith and fit you to bear witness to the truth of the gospel'. In truth, though, like the instruction to 'admonish' God's people, there seems to be a widespread tacit agreement to neglect this duty. At some points in the Church's history it was taken for granted that clergy (like the gentlemen they were) would have leisure for intellectual pursuits, theological or otherwise. Now, however, cramming the clerical diary has become the latest version of justification by works, so that time for study has been pruned even more savagely than time for prayer. Could it be, then, that the idea of the scholar priest has become as antique as that of the holy priest? I hope not.

As trainee preachers at theological college we were warned that resorting to etymology was generally a bad idea, but I think it is worth a brief excursus to uncover the roots of 'scholarship', which lie in the Greek scholē ('leisure, rest, ease'). It can be seen in Plato, for example, that scholē was time held apart from other activities, not for idleness, or for the acquisition of skills, or for other utilitarian pursuits, but for the cultivation of an examined life. This is surely a *sine qua non* of ordained ministry: the *parson* is supposed to be a representative *person* – a 'walking sacrament' of what it means to live consciously under God.[20] Deliberate patterns of scholē should be habitual for all ministers; but this does not exhaust the importance of study to deepen faith and prepare for witness, which I take to

20 Austin Farrer, 'Walking Sacraments' in *The Essential Sermons*, ed. Leslie Houlden (London: SPCK, 1991), ch. 26.

mean the study of *theology*, however diffusely or eccentrically this may be interpreted.

I said earlier that theology serves to displace the self. This is perhaps less self-evident than is the case with prayer and worship, until we perceive the true dynamic of theology, in which truth is *disclosed* (by God) rather than *attained* (by human effort): 'Theology is ... openness to a reality that gives itself away but remains ever wondrously ungraspable.'[21] For a few clergy theological scholarship may result in tangible fruit in the form of published work. But it is important, I think, to put a bracket around this, which often represents a particular vocation, and can have two baneful effects: it can open a channel for the incessant demand for greater productivity that is characteristic of the modern academy, and it can intimidate everyone else into leaving theology to the 'experts'. In any case, the greatest theologians have always understood that theology is fundamentally a spiritual discipline, and that 'the deepest truth of the one they seek to understand is only expressible ... in the transformation of their own lives'.[22] The 'theological virtues', faith, hope and love, are both the condition and the promise of theological life, and the lifeblood of the Church.

At the start of this chapter I noted Pridmore's view that 'conscientious clergy are burdened more by the contradictions of their work than by its volume'. This contradiction lies in the sense that the very things ministers are nurtured in and set apart for, like prayer, worship and theology, are often valued less than activities that are common to all people. It is very welcome, therefore, to hear that Archbishop Justin's first priority is 'the renewal of prayer and the Religious Life'.[23] It is simply not enough to meet the present crisis (*krisis*) with management, in an attempt to control it, mitigate its consequences and find a clever way out. If it is right to think of the Church

21 Mark A. McIntosh, *Divine Teaching* (Oxford: Blackwell, 2008), p. 18.

22 McIntosh, *Divine Teaching*, p. 6.

23 Justin Welby, 'ABC's first priority: The Renewal of Prayer and the Religious Life', *New Wine Magazine*, no. 58 (Summer 2013), p. 42.

as a supernatural body, not just a human organization, then its renewal will not come without the kind of openness to grace that follows a penitent awareness of our lack of sufficiency. This is surely the heart of it all, that God does for us what we could never conceive, let alone do for ourselves. In other words, vision and strategy have their limitations.

The next ten years will be a time of major change for the Church of England. Many things now taken for granted will become a distant dream. This cannot be avoided – as we often hear these days, 'doing nothing is not an option'. National church officers and diocesan bishops are rightly taking the initiative and developing ideas for growth. Parishes and deaneries are also finding creative ways to reshape local church life. I intend to take a full part in this work, though I am anxious about it too.

I have expressed concern about the Church's response to current pressures and shortages. Anxiety about decline and loss is understandable, but there is more than one way in which the Church can be diminished. After all, the Church's history is littered with lost treasures, now all but forgotten, just as her graveyards are full of once indispensable people. Death is not our final enemy.

Experience of inner-city ministry has shown me how tempting it is to put the greater part of my faith in human resourcefulness. This is a sign of the limited horizons in which I often work. Instead of placing my story, and the story of my church, within the great biblical and catholic narrative of creation, redemption and the eschaton, I find myself drawn into the smaller, narrower perspective of calculated viability, which tends to value my endeavours only in functional, instrumental terms, and seeks to stay in control. When everything is stretched and fragile, and there is so much to do, it is hard to entrust myself to the utility-resistant rule of grace. But, if the priest's role is to 'make present' divine judgement, mercy and love, there is no scriptural or theological warrant for thinking that God's presence will more likely be found in a neat management solution than a total failure and collapse. Which suggests that the anxiety I and many others experience is largely about penultimate rather than ultimate concerns. It is not our job to save the Church. If we must have a strategy – and I'm sure we must – then it must be self-effacing, or else it may actually subvert what it claims to promote. A test for this might perhaps include the question whether whatever is proposed will leave clergy more or less able and encouraged to devote time and energy to such things as prayer, worship and study – the very things for which they were set apart by ordin-ation. Such an ambitious vision might engender a new level of holiness among the clergy. At the very least it would help me to feel less burdened by the contradictions of my work. May the psalmist have the last word:

> Unless the LORD builds the house,
>   those who build it labour in vain.
> Unless the LORD guards the city,
>   the guard keeps watch in vain.
> It is in vain that you rise up early
>   and go late to rest,
> eating the bread of anxious toil;
>   for he gives sleep to his beloved.[24]

---

24 Ps. 127.1–2.

Resurrection:
The Holy People of God

SARAH COAKLEY

Cambridge and Ely

Sarah Coakley perceives the resurrection of the people of God to be revealed in a shared commitment to prayer and to the vowed life, a leaven in communities which allows the kingdom of heaven to spread and grow within the kingdom of this earth.

An elderly former parishioner of mine is dying of terminal, metastasized, cancer – it has spread now into his liver and spine: it will not be long. On my most recent visit he greets me with a newly learned joke that has been amusing him:

> *Ancient patient in hospital bed, to consultant*: 'Doctor, doctor, shall I ever recover?'
> *Consultant*: 'Yes, my dear man, you will most certainly recover. It just may not be in your lifetime.'

'It's a good one, isn't it?' says my old friend. 'Have you heard it before?' (I haven't). 'You should use it in one of your sermons' (I will). I am touched by his combination of British dark humour, full acceptance of his own fate, and sustaining Christian hope in the life to come. And I perceive something else is happening to him – for there is a dimension of his skin, though tinged with jaundice, that is already slightly luminous. One sees this sometimes in the dying, though not often: this man is actively and cooperatively *doing* his dying with Christ, letting go past resentment and future anxiety, savouring each day, each moment, for what it is: 'Look thy last on all things lovely'. The Spirit is at work. If this is death unfolding before my eyes, then it is also and already a shining intimation of resurrection. I am rendered curiously exhilarated, joyful, just by being with this man, although his prognosis is medically hopeless.

In something of that same spirit this book has been concerned with what may be dying in the parishes of the Church of England in this generation and what may be luminously coming to birth again through that death. Not everything that we see stirring in the Spirit may come to fruition 'in our lifetime'; but that does not invalidate its fecundity. As Jessica Martin reminded us at the start of this volume, the Church of England has passed through many such 'dying' transitions, some of them even more dramatic than today's (only think of the Civil War and its aftermath). Necessarily any such passage of change involves frailty and vulnerability; necessarily it demands some new ways of thinking and doing. Yet above all, and especially today, it requires discernment: it is no longer possible to effect a romantic return to the bucolic parochial idyll that George Herbert described (and which possibly never even really existed in precisely that form); nor can one grasp at an instantaneous reversal of the supposed effects of 'secularization' through merely eye-catching missiological manoeuvres. Yet that acknowledgement does not *invalidate* either traditional Anglican priestly disciplines or the necessary pressures of contemporary evangelism. The members of the Littlemore Group have staunchly resisted the polarization of these options. And as this book has also repeatedly pointed out, today's 'secularization' is in any case partial and ambiguous, masking a paradoxical remnant of the 'sacred canopy' for which there are numerous remaining signs of longing. But the strains at the moment on the parochial clergy to perform with more manifest 'success' than most feel they can attain are intense, especially in the newly extended multiple-parish benefices of the rural areas, or the run-down urban churches of the inner city; and this book has not shirked from describing these strains, with humour as well as with a certain poignant clarity. Yet it has also noted the signs of the Spirit's blowing most surprisingly 'where it wills'. It is important to remember that in an established Church 'staying' with the people of this country is itself a virtue, and a cause for hope through 'endurance' and the sustaining of 'character' (see Rom. 5.3–5).

So the authors of this book have squarely faced the (much publicized) contemporary crisis of an ageing church population and of failing church finances. But we have also gently pushed back against the fashionable presumption that *only* business models can fix such a malaise (however enlightening their analyses may be). For it is all too easy to succumb to the panic and anxiety created by interminable financial and bureaucratic demands (both ecclesiastical and legal), and of actual threats of church closure – which in some cases may indeed have to come. At the same time there is the pressure to adopt forms of mission nearly devoid of spiritual content, in a false attempt to placate or amuse, or simply to raise funds. (It is worth remembering that in the past it has always been the *theologically* sustaining 'fresh expressions' that have energized and survived: only think of early Methodism in the eighteenth century, or of the birth of the Oxford Movement in the nineteenth century.) Underlyingly, however, there is the yet deeper danger for today's clergy of sheer despair and exhaustion, of strength being stretched beyond reasonable limits, undermining health and hope. Worst of all, and even more insidiously, there lurks another threat: of the creeping erosion, under the impact of incessant overwork and worry, of commitment to prayer, always the sustaining matrix of any creative priestly life. Whenever we think of the priests who have profoundly influenced and blessed us, is it not their prayer that we realize in retrospect was emanating from them?

Archbishop Justin Welby wrote a memo early on in his archepiscopate, entitled 'ABC's first priority: The Renewal of Prayer and the Religious Life'. It starts:

When asked what my priorities are, I start with renewal of prayer and the Religious life. That is to say a commitment to encouraging Christians to pray, and the development of new forms of community where life is lived according to a shared 'rule' so that we support one another to new depths of love and obedience in our lives of faith.

At the heart of what it is to be a Christian is relationship. We have friendship with Christ and because of all that He did we build friendships with each other based in the Spirit of God working among us. So prayer is utterly crucial, and prayer as part of a community demonstrates relationship. It is a good thing in itself, and the collateral benefits in the past have been everything from overflowing new life in the church, to the renewal of civil society. There has never been a renewal of the church without a renewal of prayer and the Religious life.[1]

Archbishop Welby's vision on this score has already resulted in the creation of the Community of St Anselm at Lambeth, and the encouragement of many burgeoning local experiments in 'new monasticism'. These, and other related phenomena, will concern the Littlemore Group in its next book (*The Vowed Life*), which will focus on the various vows that Christians make in their lifetime and how they are integrally related. For there is a certain danger here of extrapolating the renewed contemporary fascination with *religious* vows away from the commitment made by all Christians in baptism (and again in confirmation) to continue to cooperate with the sanctifying grace of the Holy Spirit 'unto our lives' end'. It is in the renewed commitment to prayer, theological reflection and personal transformation of life that the Littlemore Group has always staked its hope for the Church, as the reflections in this book once again vividly demonstrate: 'There has never been a renewal of the church without a renewal of prayer ...'

---

1 Justin Welby, 'ABC's first priority: The Renewal of Prayer and the Religious Life', *New Wine Magazine*, no. 58 (Summer 2013), p. 42.

It is here indeed that 'true resurrection' will surely be found, doubtless in many different new shapes and forms, some gloriously evident already, and some (now 'growing secretly') to be made more manifest 'not in our lifetime'. But Archbishop Welby puts his finger on the key issue when he writes of the vital significance of priestly teaching and 'encouragement' in the life of prayer, and of its indispensable sustenance of 'community'. One might more probingly underscore that parish priests just as much need the *laity* to encourage and goad them in the disciplines of prayer as *vice versa*. Perhaps nowhere is this more important than in struggling little rural and urban churches, where even the daily or weekly commitment of a few laity to that sustaining incubus of prayer can have an effect that is tangible and electrifying. I recall dropping into a local suburban church a while ago, happily surprised to find its doors open. I was on my way to what I thought might be a difficult meeting at the university, and I wanted time to draw breath. As I entered the church (which appeared empty) I became aware instantly of a palpable 'presence', drawing me in. I sat down in a back pew and only after a few moments realized that a small group of lay congregants were gathered in a side chapel: they were evidently keeping a few minutes of silence after the recitation of the Lord's Prayer at the end of morning office. It was this alluring atmosphere of focused prayer that I had sensed immediately on entry, and it had already sustained my own rather fumbling petitions for the meeting I was about to attend. The silence was eventually broken as several names and petitions were read out relating to the local parish and its people. The dismissal and blessing were then quietly announced and a handful of people emerged from the chapel – mostly elderly, but one youthful. They had done their 'work' for the morning. This unostentatious duty, combining office, silence and petition, had more than adequately confirmed Christ's promise about his presence among 'two or three gathered together' (Matt. 18.20). I left the church sustained and uplifted, no longer fearful about my meeting to come. And

I have had much reason to think afresh about this small incident as the Littlemore Group has ruminated, as it does again at the start of this book, on the necessity of the renewal and deepening of prayerful lay leadership in the far-flung parishes of our country. It is the 'holy people of God' who must and will effect this renewal in the Spirit, not simply the priest – whose own prayers are in turn held to account by her praying people.

This book represents, therefore, neither a lament for a lost parochial past nor an admission of hopelessness in the face of the impossible: for, as my dying parishioner insisted, speaking of his own life to come, 'we shall [all] most certainly recover'. However searing the contemporary ecclesiastical challenges we have faced in this volume, something non-negotiable and vital endures: the celebration of the priestly *vocation* to prayer, which is by definition ever and always the laity's *invitation* to prayer. It is to this 'one thing necessary' that the writers of this book have once again clung – *For God's Sake*, and for the sake of the future Church of England.

Afterword

ROWAN WILLIAMS

Cambridge

I read these essays at about the same time as I was completing some work on Bonhoeffer's *Ethics* – a book that could do with revisiting. Bonhoeffer in these late, fragmentary essays and drafts is already moving in the direction of the prison letters, with their impatience and ambivalence about the Church in self-defensive mode (even when defending itself against a manifest evil like the Aryan laws of the Third Reich). The Church, he says in effect, can't help taking up space in the world; but the key point is that it takes up space not for itself but for the world's sake. It doesn't occupy a territory that it has to police, but tries to guarantee a place where human beings may encounter and experience their humanity. It does so not out of any sentimental belief in the glory of the human spirit as such, but because God has been seen and heard in a life lived in complete solidarity with humanity – and specifically with lost and failing humanity. To be 'with God' or 'in Christ' is to be with and in this act of solidarity. And solidarity cannot be expressed if the central question is about controlling a defined religious space in the social world. The Church is visible, tangible, taking up space, yet always insisting that that space is everyone's. The Church's resistance to the order of the 'world' is not a contest for dominance but a stubborn refusal to accept terms for human destiny or dignity that are defined by anything less than the divine gift and call.

Echoes of this abound in these pages. Running through many of these reflections is the theme of being-with, accompanying: to use a phrase I've used elsewhere, it's as though our society retains an awkward and inarticulate sense of a church-shaped gap, even a priest-shaped gap in the social scene. What are we there for? To guarantee that there is room for something not very fully or articulately understood, but something we write off at our peril. Not a superstitious anxiety or a hankering after magic, though these things will surface at times; much more a passion to know that some sort of connection is being kept open on everyone's behalf. Hence the frustrating, tantalizing moments when priestly ministry genuinely and unmistakably touches people in their depths without – apparently – suggesting to anyone that the proper response is commitment, regular belonging. What these writers say here shows an exemplary sensitivity to this, keeping a careful eye on the temptation to improve occasions, exploit contacts, force paces. Evidently for a lot of people a lot of the time, what matters is the basic assurance that the channels are still open; the ironic implication for the priest is often that trying to push individuals through the channels, so to speak, chokes the flow and makes people see the door as closed.

This shouldn't mean (and it clearly doesn't for the contributors to this book) that our identity as Church is passive, simply being custodians of a potentially life-giving space. What we read about is much more a series of attempts to think imaginatively about how that space is reshaped, made more fully visible; how the ministers of the gospel quietly observe and identify where the need for space arises; how they develop a nose for closed and stifling atmospheres and learn how to indicate a larger room to inhabit. It's helpful to read reflections that don't see 'Fresh Expressions' as somehow bound in to aggressive, consumerized recruiting strategies: most such enterprises are essentially attempts to find where people need 'air'. And it is also noticeable how in these pages there are frequent acknowledgements of those encounters where people uncommitted to the Church show with complete clarity in their acts and encounters how life-giving space might be given and inhabited. 'Anxiety' may be a word that recurs in these essays, but it is recognized for what it is and faced down: the longing to control outcomes and the panic that supervenes when we can't is identified as one of the major obstacles to the offer we are there to make.

'Dancing faster' is indeed the temptation. The ministry that is evoked in this book is one that seeks above all to allow God to be God, and not to suppose that our intensity of feeling, planning or talking will automatically make room for the divine act in the way that is most necessary and most life-giving. But it is also surely a ministry that looks to generate in the entire community the same attunement to this basic need for space, this solidarity in watching for the places where the human landscape is being eroded. Not a lot can be said in favour of a new clericalism that leaves the priest as a solitary virtuoso of discernment. But one thing that emerges from these pages is that the opposite of clericalism is not spreading the load of Things To Do but working on the assumption that the priest's discernment can help to create discernment in the community – the discernment, patience and acute diagnostic sense for what humanly matters. And the priest's regular prayer – so intensely at the centre of the ministry of those who have written here, so effectively underlined in the model of new monastic community – is a visible sign and reminder of where discernment has to be anchored, in patience in the presence of God.

Asking an institution to go on supporting a practice that is detached about certain sorts of outcome, unworried about control and hopeful rather than obsessional about growing in numbers is asking a lot; and there are a good few people in the Church of England today who would say that it is asking too much or asking the wrong thing. There are perfectly real questions about accountability and strategy to be asked. But our writers are concerned not to let themselves be moved too far from theology; and this entails not being moved too far from the register of symbol. Sense is made and preserved by the creation of words, images, histories and geographies; bits of the material environment continue to speak even when the full, articulate contexts in which they were first shaped have faded. And the central symbol for Christian faith remains that extraordinary and still potentially shocking sign of divine solidarity, the cross of Jesus. Letting God's solidarity with us make sense of who and what we are, in the way Bonhoeffer is feeling for, is the calling that the minister of the gospel has accepted. The priest and the Church overall are to stay there, under that sign, wherever they literally find themselves, in order to say something about the solidarity of God, and this must somehow be the touchstone of what we are trying to achieve, locally and not so locally, in pastoral strategy. And it doesn't hurt to remind ourselves also of the character of Jesus' own activity: he attends to what is needed ('What do you want me to do for you?'); he offers the possibility of a transition into another kind of life (healed, forgiven, reintegrated in community, conscious that God hears); he leaves open also the possibility of non-response ('Were not ten healed? Where are the nine?'). His presence emphatically changes things, alters the shape of the world; but not as a programme recruiting supporters. It is disciples – learners – that he invites rather than 'supporters', members of a human society ('membership' in Christ's Body is another thing entirely). What lessons might we draw from that?

The history of the Church of England so far refuses to die quietly – that history of being relied on to provide a place or a connection, irrespective of the number of conversions or commitments. God forbid that we forget about conversion and commitment; there is a fullness, a passion, of adherence in which we believe human beings find themselves most comprehensively. But all the reflections here circle back towards the question of what kinds of ordinary human trust and companionship have to be sustained for this language to take any root, for it to mean something more than just recruitment. The

Church's credibility is not first and foremost the plausibility of what it says, nor the exemplary lives of its members or its clergy (thank goodness), but its capacity to show that there is a space into which humans can grow. For this it needs a ministry that is as patient and as realistic as those described here; it needs ministers who believe in God, and believe that God is indeed God, and that therefore they don't have to be God.

> The church is nothing but that piece of humanity where Christ really has taken form ... The church is the human being who has become human, has been judged, and has been awakened to new life in Christ. Therefore essentially its first concern is not with the so-called religious functions of human beings, but with the existence in the world of whole human beings in all their relationships.[1]

Bonhoeffer is far from reducing the Church to a 'secular' shape; quite the contrary. But the 'awakened' life that the gospel offers, dramatically different and more expansive in comparison with what we think of as routine human existence, comes to birth unpredictably – sometimes gradually, sometimes painfully rapidly (think of the parables of the kingdom in the Gospels). This deeply Christologically grounded perspective is as vital as anything could be for our future as a Church that is somehow the form of divine solidarity, the form taken by Christ. And it is kept alive for us only by the constant exposure that is prayer.

---

1 Dietrich Bonhoeffer, *Ethics* (Minneapolis, MN: Fortress Press, 2005), p. 97.

Note on the Conference

This book finds its remote origins in a conference held in September 2011 at Lichfield Cathedral which sought to consider the place of the 'Scholar Priest' in today's Anglican Church. Participants were: Pete Wilcox, Frances Ward, Andrew Shanks, Alex Hughes, Sister Judith SLG, Matt Bullimore, Edmund Newey, Rachel Mann, Ian Wallis, Jessica Martin, Victoria Johnson and Sarah Coakley. The poet Michael Symmons-Roberts was present for part of the conference and gave a reading from recent work; musicians from the Close gave a short evening concert.

In the intervening years the book has been most decisively shaped by the personal experience of contributors in the context of a fast-changing ministerial landscape within the Church of England.